CAREE~ FOR

GOURMETS
& Others Who Relish Food

Mary Donovan

Second Edition

VGM Career Books

Chicago New York San Francisco Lisbon London Madrid Mexico City
Milan New Delhi San Juan Seoul Singapore Sydney Toronto

VGM Career Books

A Division of The **McGraw·Hill** Companies

1 2 3 4 5 6 7 8 9 0   LBM/LBM   1 0 9 8 7 6 5 4 3 2

ISBN 0-07-138729-3 (hardcover)
      0-07-138728-5 (paperback)

This book was set in Goudy Old Style by ImPrint Services
Printed and bound by Lake Book Manufacturing

McGraw-Hill books are available at special quantity discounts to use as premiums and sales promotions, or for use in corporate training programs. For more information, please write to the Director of Special Sales, Professional Publishing, McGraw-Hill, Two Penn Plaza, New York, NY 10121-2298. Or contact your local bookstore.

This book is printed on acid-free paper.

To my dear family: Thomas,
Connor, Bronwyn,
Molly, and Daphne

Contents

Foreword

Are there opportunities in the food industry? I say there are. Just fifty years ago, it was not considered a good idea for a young person to contemplate a career in cooking. Agriculture, yes, but not in the preparation of food or in the few elements that made up the food industry at that time. As a nation, our interest in good food has increased dramatically, and it will continue to increase. We are no longer a nation of meat, potatoes, and apple pie eaters. We want good vegetables and fruit, good cheese, and good prepared products.

How has all of this evolved? First of all, it was the passion shared by a few food enthusiasts such as Julia Child, James Beard, Craig Claiborne, Elizabeth David, and Alice Waters. All of them were exposed to the foods of France and Italy and decided that America needed change in its eating habits. And change it has had! Many young people today share that passion and are finding satisfying and rewarding careers—not just cooking, but in all parts of the food industry: writing, teaching, catering, small specialized agriculture, as well as baking and candy or jam making.

Five years ago would you have thought that Italian-type biscotti, made by small bakers, would be available in every specialized food shop in America? Or that small farmer's markets would again be the way to get fresher fruit and vegetables? There are many changes taking place in what we eat, where we eat, and who provides our food. It all depends on people with a passion for food and the will to share it with others.

Chuck Williams
Founder, Vice-Chairman of the Board
Williams-Sonoma, Inc.

CHAPTER ONE

Jobs for Gourmets

Y ou've planned the menu, shopped at the best markets for fruits, vegetables, fresh herbs, seafood, and meats. You've scoured the town, or developed a network of mail-order and on-line sources, to be certain that you can produce one of the finest cups of coffee, espresso, or even cappuccino on your block. Your dinner parties are considered one of the best shows in town. And, invariably, when you serve the grand finale, at least one person at the table will sigh, lean back, and say:

"You really should own your own restaurant."

The notion of working with food for a living is one that almost always finds its way into the heart and soul of anyone who truly savors fine food, fine wine, fine teas and coffees, and the physical and emotional act of dining well. This is a true gourmet. No facet of food is dull to gourmets, with their voracious appetites for the best, the most magnificent, the finest. (A gourmet should not be confused, of course, with a gourmand, an entirely separate type of being whose main comfort derives from gargantuan portions of good food, consumed at regular intervals, the more closely spaced the better.)

Now, of course, there will be variations on the generic brand of gourmet. And whether it is possible, or desirable, to surrender your unencumbered passion for fine food to the more humdrum aspects of earning your living by cooking will depend on you. Should you jump ship from the mainstream workaday world into the field of cooking?

In some ways, this field is one of the most tolerant of the individual. People are still able to create their own niches by providing very specialized services. And when you arrive at this career with experience from another trade, it is often possible to meld the two paths into one. The talents and skills you may have developed in a seemingly unrelated field are often the very ones that will give you a special advantage in the hospitality industry.

You may stumble upon your true vocation only after spending a number of years as an accountant, a teacher, a computer programmer, an editor, or a mechanic. Or, you may have always known, from the time you were old enough to bang a spoon inside a pot and dream of baking pies all by yourself. No matter where you come from, there is a common ground for all gourmets: the love of fine food and wine.

Getting a start in any career takes some definite steps. It's not always necessary to complete each and every one of these steps in the exact sequence outlined here. Some steps may be optional; there are relatively few absolute requirements in this field beyond the willingness to always strive for the best possible quality.

The Chef's Role

Chefs have been associated with power and privilege throughout history. The power was not always held by the chefs, however. As soon as a society advanced enough to establish a formal power structure, the nobility very often put their wealth and power on prominent display by owning or employing the best chef possible. A talented chef captured as a slave through foreign conquest was a highly valued war prize in many countries.

Not all those who worked with food for a living were slaves, of course. Louis XIV had a very special group of around five hundred whose sole responsibility was to produce and serve meals to the king and his court. These positions were held by noblemen who paid for the privilege of serving the king.

As the feudal system began to break down, and a more democratic society with a middle class began to evolve, the chef's role changed. In 1765, the owner of a Paris café, who is known today only by the name Boulanger, won a historic court case against the caterer's guild. Until this time, a café owner such as Monsieur Boulanger was entitled to serve his guests only drinks and "restorative broths." Any prepared foods served hot had to come from a caterer. When Boulanger chose to offer his guests a dish of sheep's feet that he himself had stewed in a white sauce, he was taken to court by the guild of caterers. The court ruled that, as they did not consider this dish a stew, Boulanger had not violated the law. As time passed, this first restaurateur continued to expand his menu.

This pivotal event defined the new role of the chef and signaled the birth of the modern restaurant. It also marked the beginning of a time when guests could have a meal somewhere other than in an inn or from a caterer. And, for the first time, the fine cuisine that was previously the exclusive privilege of the elite was available to greater numbers of people of all classes.

The first restaurants were more like men's clubs than any restaurant we would be familiar with today. Women of good society simply did not enter them. Two of the most famous members of this profession, Auguste Escoffier and Cesar Ritz, were the ones to finally smash this tradition. They introduced dining rooms that were attractively lit, with lovely table settings, and made the restaurant of the Savoy Hotel an acceptable place to be seen for both men and women of good reputation.

Today, when the culinary arts come under discussion, the picture that comes to mind first is the chef for a restaurant, dressed in a white jacket, checkered pants, and wearing a *toque blanche* (the tall, pleated, white chef's hat). And today, the chef that comes to mind may be male or female and from almost any country in the world. Times have definitely changed in the world of culinary arts.

The Professional Culinarian

When you read about hot new chefs in a food magazine or the Wednesday edition of the paper, it is more and more common to find that they attended school to learn their craft. They speak of their work as a profession, and they act in a manner befitting the profession with only a few, short-lived phenomena to break the rule. The term *culinarian* is a badge of honor to most of its practitioners. So, it is sometimes hard to remember that working as a chef was once not as respectable as working in a "real profession" such as teaching, law, or medicine.

It may be that people used to equate work in the service industry with being someone's servant. Our democratic nation promoted the idea that we all should be masters, and that those who held themselves in high esteem could not retain a sense of dignity while working at the beck and call of someone else. This attitude has gradually changed. Chefs, caterers, pastry chefs, and others who work in the culinary arts are becoming the darlings of the media. The chef is often regarded as a glamorous superstar, much as an actor might be.

One reason chefs are enjoying greater prestige is that Americans have become increasingly sophisticated about the kinds of foods they enjoy eating. People who would have never traveled to Italy, France, or the Pacific Islands in the normal course of events forty or fifty years ago may now be able to visit these exotic climes. There, they may find themselves eating strange new foods and discovering they enjoy these new dishes as much as the foods they grew up on. This taste for new foods can develop just as easily when people travel from region to region within their own borders as it does during international travel.

What this awareness of different ethnic cuisines has meant to the restaurant industry can hardly be overstated. The last few decades have ushered in waves of new restaurants. For the first time since such records have been kept, Mexican restaurants have edged out other restaurants of all sorts as the number one favorite. Salsa has even outstripped ketchup as the top-selling condiment.

Conversely, American culinary pride, first awakened from a deep sleep a couple of decades ago, continues to blossom. Parts of the country previously unknown for anything other than macadamia nuts or peanuts have become famous for the gourmet specialties of the region. Entire issues of such respected magazines as *Food & Wine* are sometimes dedicated to the cuisines of the Chesapeake Bay area or Hawaii. This new awareness of the pleasures of food means more people are eating more meals away from their homes with every passing year. In fact, America's interest in eating out has increased steadily since the years following World War II, when Americans experienced a simultaneous increase in disposable income and in the amount of time spent away from the home as the two-income family became the norm.

All this interest in fine cuisine means lots of jobs for gourmets.

Do You Have What It Takes?

Today, any career choice is difficult, and it is a serious challenge to make an objective and carefully thought-out decision about anything that will have far-reaching effects on the rest of your life. There is no completely accurate personality test that will unveil your perfect job. What does help is to take careful stock of what you know about yourself and how your personal traits stack up against some of the harsher realities of the culinary arts.

Will You Be Happy Working with Food Every Single Day?

Most, though not all, jobs in the culinary arts involve cooking. Try to be as realistic as possible about how you would feel, cooking all day long, every single day. Not every aspect of cooking is fun. A lot of the work is tedious and repetitive. And when you first start in this field, the most tedious and repetitive chores will most likely be your lot. If you do the work well and are diligent, you will probably move on fairly quickly to more rewarding jobs. Still, there will always be onions to peel and chop, carrots to slice, stocks to prepare, and shrimp to peel and devein. Virtually every chef has to do at least some of the "prep" work before he or she tackles the more glamorous job of preparing an actual dish for a guest.

Another thing to remember is that when you are planning and preparing dinner parties, you can select just those foods that please you and skip those that you find less appetizing. You won't have that luxury if you become a professional. Even though you may have a lifelong prejudice against salmon or lamb, there is a high probability that you will find yourself preparing it somewhere during the course of your career.

You must be able to find pleasure in food, in the way it looks, tastes, feels, the sounds it makes as it is cut and as it cooks, and the way that it looks on the plate just before it is whisked away to the guest. This is just as important if you are serving the foods as if you are cooking them. The waiter is often responsible for helping guests make a decision about a meal, and no matter who might be responsible for the success or failure of a meal, guests will usually remember the waiter as holding the key to their dinnertime fate.

Are You Confident You Can Work with Others as Part of a Team?

Even though most people arrive at the culinary arts as a career choice out of a love for food and cooking, it is just as important, perhaps more so, to enjoy working for the happiness and satisfaction of someone else. That someone else is the guest. It is probably a good idea to use that exact word and not client, customer, or patron. Referring to those who ultimately pay your salary as guests puts them into a special category. At its most basic, the "team" is a partnership between you and the guest.

As you first start out, perhaps in a catering house where you peel seemingly endless mountains of carrots, cut up more chickens than you ever knew existed, and bake enough cakes to make you swear off dessert for the rest of your life, it might be difficult to visualize the guest that you never actually get to see. If you can keep that individual in mind as the person who is going to be enjoying a salad that you made possible at a wedding reception, you will have a head start.

Sometimes, it is easier to stay motivated by the thought of the guests when they don't get very close. Dining room and banquet hall managers often have a challenge when faced with guests who can't make up their minds or who insist on daffodils in November. But, almost anyone who has made a mark in this field, whether at work in the kitchen or the dining room, truly enjoys working with people.

The kitchen and the dining room are generally not staffed by one single person, so it is important to be able to work side by side with other people on a daily basis. Very often, the actual work space that you must share will be tight. If you have any doubt, visit a busy restaurant on a Saturday night, and look through the doors of the kitchen, or wander by the waiters' station.

This work is both physical and mental, and it is definitely demanding. When you find yourself stressed to your limit, you need maturity and calmness to dig down a little deeper and find the energy to keep going without throwing a tantrum. Those legends about famous chefs and maître d's who ruled their domains through tantrums, bullying, and intimidation are becoming a part of ancient culinary lore. Today's kitchen and dining room must be as efficiently run as possible to attract a clientele that will return over and over again. No one wants to go back to a restaurant that has scared waiters spilling drinks and acting distracted, or that has meals coming out late, cold, or burned because the cooks can't concentrate on their work for fear that the chef will explode over some trivial detail.

Of course, not everyone who chooses this field winds up working in a kitchen or a dining room. There are numerous other opportunities, which will be discussed in detail later in this book. Some of these careers will also involve close work with a team or a group of clients. There are other jobs in which you can work by yourself for the majority of the time. But even if you have a more solitary career in this field, you need to be able to work with others to some degree, whether it is working with just your literary agent and an editor, or trying to sell your new design for a kitchen tool. For most of us, teamwork is a skill that can be (and must be) enhanced though constant practice, attention, and effort. Certainly, with all of the stress that comes along with a career in cooking, one should expect that things may sometimes get a little wild. These episodes should never topple over into frenzy, however.

Do You Have an Artist Within?

Americans have become more sophisticated about food. They are more conscious than ever not only about what tastes good, but about what looks good. Photographs of foods found in the living sections of general interest magazines and newspapers have become just as beautiful and elegant as those found in publications devoted strictly to food. The number of gourmets is growing, and this offers a wonderful challenge to the chef.

A certain flair, a knack for combining interesting colors, textures, and temperatures on a single plate, and a talent for balancing on that fine line between faddish and trendy are all tricks that are found in the bag of the truly talented chef. There won't always be someone standing at your shoulder, asking you if you remembered to put the garnish on the plate, or reminding you that the carrots go on the left and the sauce on the bottom.

It is important to have a vivid appreciation of beautiful things so that you can begin to draw inspiration from what is around you. This doesn't mean that you should paint pictures on the plate or play elaborate or tortured games with foods simply to create an effect. Certain fundamental rules about contrast and similarity are known to work when composing a menu or a single recipe. The overall dictum is to retain a sense of balance, allowing the special qualities of food to speak for themselves. This is a subtle, complex issue, even for those who spend years working with foods.

The artist's tools of balance, simplicity, harmony, contrast, perfect surprise, and satisfaction are paired with seamless technique in creating a masterpiece in any craft. These ideals are impossible to define exactly, but as skill and experience are accumulated, they do become easier to recognize, and to produce.

How Do You Feel About Working on Holidays?

Working in a restaurant involves hard physical labor. You will be on your feet, moving, lifting heavy pots or loaded trays, whipping, kneading, pounding, cutting, and slicing for several hours. It is not uncommon to have to work ten, twelve, or even more hours in a row from time to time. This is certainly one of the most unglamorous aspects of this career. The work is exhausting and grueling, and, more often than not, you will be tired, dirty, and worn out at the end of a shift.

Whether you are the pantry cook who makes all the salads or the executive chef who makes all the decisions, there will be times when you simply have to grit your teeth and do the pots because the dishwasher didn't come in to work. Or, you must peel the garlic because it has to be done, and there is no one else. You need a great deal of willpower, stamina, and a special reserve of emotional strength to keep going one more hour or one more shift.

As high as you may climb in this field, there are always days when you will wonder why you ever chose a job that keeps you from joining in with family celebrations like Thanksgiving, Fourth of July, and Mother's Day. Holidays are often the busiest times for restaurants, and if the reservation book shows one hundred guests or more, chances are good that you will have to be there, doing your job, in a hot room with no windows. You may wonder at that moment why you ever thought you would like to cook for a living. But remember, there truly is no more satisfying work, if you really love to cook.

Jobs and Schools

Having looked over a short laundry list of the common complaints of those who actually work in kitchens and dining rooms throughout the land, you now have a better notion of whether you might be suited to this type of job. The next step is to get involved in it, in some way, as a paid worker. Whether you are still in school or still in your original career, there is usually a part-time job in a restaurant, hospital, cafeteria, pizza parlor, or hamburger stand that can accommodate your schedule. If you don't have any experience at all, don't be too surprised if the four-star restaurants in town aren't eager to hire you as the sous-chef. Look for the best job you can find, but remember that you must start somewhere.

This first plunge into the food service industry will give you valuable insights and information for the future. Even if all you come away with from your first encounter is a passing familiarity with some of the lingo and a callus from peeling carrots for six hours straight, you will have begun the process of learning about food, cooking, and restaurants. That process will never end. Even the most famous gourmets are as eager as anyone else to try something completely new, to experience a flavor that is unique, a dish that is the essence of what cooking should be. This is the delight in food that got you started, and it is the light that will guide you through your career. But you are responsible for feeding the delight and nurturing it carefully through the years.

Another important step you might want to take is enrolling in a cooking class or attending cooking demonstrations. There are a variety of educational programs available devoted to the culinary arts. The type of education and training best suited to a person looking forward to a career in the culinary arts usually differs from the program prescribed for other fields. Rather than spending many hours in a library doing term papers and preparing to defend a thesis, you will most likely get the bulk of your education hands-on in a kitchen by cooking food, tasting it, and putting it on plates, under the direction of your teacher.

This is not to say that there is no theory involved in cooking. There is, and it is fascinating. Writers such as Harold McGee, author of *Kitchen Science: The Myth and Lore of Cooking* and *The Curious Cook*, have turned their keen eyes on the more technical aspects of cooking and made it not only understandable but exciting. Studying culinary theory can be a truly interesting part of one's education and indispensable for anyone who wants to be fully versed in cooking. And at least one renowned university, Boston University, offers a master's program in liberal arts devoted to gastronomy. According to the *Oxford English Dictionary*, gastronomy is "the art and science of delicate eating." What could be more cerebral than that?

Back to practical matters, however, it must be noted that cooking at home is not the same thing as cooking in a restaurant, which is the skill that you need to learn if you are going to become a chef. Cooking can be learned, and proficiency at the craft is gained through constant practice and study. The type of course you take will be determined by how much time you have to devote to this type of study, as well as how much money you can afford to invest.

High school programs in vocational schools are a good choice for those who know that they want to work with food while they are still in secondary school. Many of these courses are excellent and offer a well-rounded introduction to basic cooking skills, the proper service of food, fundamentals of sanitation and safety in the kitchen, and various managerial aspects of the food service industry. Baking and pastry courses may also be offered to further refine the educational program.

If you are out of school, or if you are studying in another program but have a definite desire to learn more, there are additional opportunities. Adult education courses offered through high schools, vocational schools, junior colleges, and cooking schools are a fertile ground. The range of subjects is extensive, from vegetarian cuisine to candy making. It is usually easy to find a class that interests you, whether you want to learn fundamental skills such as the proper preparation of stocks, soups, or basic sauces or do more advanced work to prepare to compete in food shows.

Other ways to find beneficial classes are to look for courses offered at cookware supply stores, gourmet shops, or department stores. Several private schools also offer courses throughout the country. Some of the more famous are those offered by noted chefs and cookbook authors such as Betty Rosbottom at La Belle Pomme in Columbus, Ohio.

In larger cities, there are often series of demonstrations by famous chefs. These may be provided in conjunction with food festivals and other community celebrations, or they may be tied in with local farmer's markets. Keep a keen eye out, and read the local paper thoroughly.

If you have tried several classes, found a job in a restaurant, and are still eager for more, then it is time to consider a more formal education offered at one of the more than three thousand cooking schools throughout the United States alone. There are more schools in Europe, Canada, and elsewhere, to be sure, such as the Cordon Bleu in London and LaVarenne in Paris. Journeying to such interesting and dynamic centers may be an exciting way to further your education. But, if you will most likely be remaining in the States, it is fair to say that your choices are at least as good as if you had all the world from which to select.

The number of recognized schools that offer programs for professional cooks and chefs is growing each year. In fact, it might seem as if the supply of schools will shortly outstrip the number of available students, but it is important to remember that the food service industry is still growing, and it shows little sign of stopping soon. Current figures, according to the National Restaurant Association, indicate that the food service industry will be in need of 12.5 million workers by the year 2008. Doubtless, there will be room for you.

Some schools for the professionals offer programs that last from one month to three months. When you finish, you will have a certificate of completion or a diploma. Others offer a more complete course of study that lasts a year or more, resulting in an associate's degree. Still other schools offer a bachelor's degree after four years of study; the Culinary Institute, for example, offers two-year associate's degrees and four-year bachelor's programs in either baking and pastry or culinary arts.

Evaluating Schools

There are a number of things to consider when choosing a school. First, how much time can you afford to devote to your education? If you have no one to take care of but yourself, you may be able to stop working and devote yourself fully to school for the time that it takes to reach your personal goal. However, anyone who has family obligations might need to give it more careful thought. Most good schools do offer financial aid, of course. If you need to work while you are in school, then it might be helpful to find a school that does not have an extremely strenuous curriculum that requires you to be in class for eight hours a day with a few additional hours of study required beyond that.

For the truly motivated individual, nothing is more exhilarating than finding a school that plunges you into the world of food and cooking. Visiting prospective schools can be a lot of fun. When you do go on a tour, look around carefully and ask some specific questions. How large is the faculty, and what are their credentials? Some schools have only one or two large demonstration kitchens. One chef demonstrates how to prepare a dish while a great many students look on, taking notes. Other schools have numerous kitchens where students are expected to work with the food themselves. The better the ratio between students and instructors, the more hands-on experience you can expect, and the more thorough your cooking education is likely to be. It is one thing to read about making a beurre blanc or a soufflé, or even to watch someone else prepare these culinary masterpieces in front of you. It is quite another to actually master the technique yourself.

There should be a logical progression to the curriculum as well. Certain fundamentals must be mastered before you are ready to move on to more advanced work. This is just as true in cooking as it is for those beginning careers in professional sports, in music, in dance, or in theater. The most basic concepts and skills should be given the biggest focus at first and then constantly reinforced throughout one's training. Learning to use a knife safely and properly is perhaps the most fundamental skill of all. The proper way to handle a knife, hone it, and sharpen it, as well as the basic cuts and their correct dimensions, are all important in the education of a chef.

Other, related subjects are of importance to the professional as well. Will you be given instruction in sanitation, safety, and nutrition? Is there at least one class devoted to product identification so that you can learn quality standards?

The chef must have a complete and virtually automatic mastery of techniques used to work with food: boiling, steaming, stewing, braising, roasting, grilling, sautéing, baking, and much more. The underlying principles of these techniques should be reinforced again and again as you advance from introductory courses to the most advanced class offered at the school. Creativity is an important part of cooking, but it flourishes most when it is cultivated in an atmosphere of professionalism.

When you look into the kitchens, try to get a sense of how much practical experience you will be getting. It isn't enough to know just a few fundamentals. Everyone should be able to properly sauté a chicken breast or broil a steak to the correct doneness. You will be called upon to perform a number of different tasks throughout your career, from boiling vegetables to creating a menu. Will you be able to get to the stove, with enough pots and pans available, to get a good hands-on experience? Look around to see how modern the equipment is, and whether or not there are conventional, convection, hearth-style, and wood-fired stoves. Not every school is able to offer every single piece of equipment, but the more the better. They will be happy to show off their high-tech tools if you ask.

Beyond the Kitchen

Even though a hands-on approach to cooking is the most effective way to master the craft, you will be learning more than simply how to process food from the delivery truck into a plated meal ready to serve the guest. There is a history to this profession and a number of aspects that are still best taught in lecture form. This means that there should be lecture halls available. In addition, an excellent school will be able to provide students with a library that features an extensive collection of books devoted to the culinary arts and related fields. A video library is also highly valuable, as are computers.

If you were to ask someone on the street how much time the average chef is likely to spend doing research, reading, or writing, the answer you got would probably be wildly inaccurate. It is impossible to keep current without putting the time and effort into "book work." There will always be new products, unfamiliar foods, exciting new twists on old standards, an intriguing cuisine that is sweeping the country seemingly overnight. A library filled with books, periodicals, journals, videos, and computer software that makes it easy to access all this new information is crucial.

When you look around the school, try to get a sense of how much pride the school takes in its facilities, its faculty, and its students. Kitchens shouldn't look like dungeons, and work areas should be well lit and safe. You will be learning more than simply how to cook at a school like this. You will also learn valuable lessons about how to keep a kitchen safe, clean, and running at top efficiency.

The more aspects of a culinary education touched on by a curriculum, the better for you. Cooking is not the be-all and end-all for most chefs. Wine appreciation, especially with a focus on wine as an accompaniment to food, is fundamental. So are courses that touch on the basics of managing a restaurant and developing a menu or a restaurant concept. Practical experience in the "front of the house," working as a waiter, maître d', or wine steward, and some basic and advanced work in baking and pastry are also invaluable parts of any in-depth culinary education.

The list goes on and on, and it is easy to see that you could spend your life studying this fascinating field. And, truly, you should! But unless you actually embark on a career, you will remain a devoted amateur. And while there is a lot to be said for getting as close to perfection in one's hobbies as possible, it isn't really what you started out to do.

Once you are ready to leave school for the "real world," you will be on the way to an even more thorough education than you could get even if you were to stay in school for decades. There is no substitute for experience. Some of the most famous chefs never have attended any formal cooking school. They gained all of their considerable expertise working under the tutelage of a real live chef. This is the famous school of "hard knocks," and most people find themselves in line for a few rude awakenings as they begin their careers. The experience is a common and important part of one's training. It is in the crucible of a professional kitchen that you will learn the skills that make a great chef out of an adequate cook. Organization, the ability to put tasks in their correct priority, and keeping track of several tasks at the same time are some of these skills. When you have torched several trays of bacon because you got busy breaking down chickens, or you let the pasta overcook for the fiftieth time because the ducks had to come out of the oven, you will probably despair of ever having the "chef's nose" that tells you to yank the pan off the fire the instant before the sauce scorches. It does come. It just doesn't develop overnight.

Switching to a Culinary Career

Today, more than ever, those entering the food service industry for the first time are coming from the ranks of some other career. Perhaps a person finally decides that this is the time to move, make that radical switch from banker to banquet chef. If you spend any amount of time talking to people who work in restaurants, it won't take very long before you find several who previously earned a living as teachers, bankers, mechanics, librarians, construction workers, or researchers.

Life experience is an invaluable commodity. Every job teaches you a little more about yourself, as well as a little more about how to work. The more you know about yourself and the way you like to work, the more confident you can be that this career choice will lead to success.

For those who have been out of the job market for some time, returning to work can be an overwhelming prospect. Men and women who have taken time away from their careers to raise their families often find themselves at a disadvantage. Even when they have impressive education and work experience to show, they may find they can't compete with younger candidates who have been in touch with the field. This often convinces them to search in a new field, perhaps one that has always held interest: professional cooking. The restaurant world is sometimes a better option than others for a first-time job seeker or someone who is returning to the field after a break of a few years. Job openings appear fairly often, and on-the-job training is usually not a problem for anyone entering in a low-level spot.

Many people also appreciate the flexibility the career offers. Those who have left the workaday world to raise families, pursue special goals, or to gain further education may wonder if there is any way to marry fulfilling work with the rest of their lives. Many industries, including this one, are finding that it makes better sense to find ways to keep their trained workers, rather than dismissing them because they have decided to have children or pursue work in another field.

The hours of this industry are so varied that it would be difficult to define typical hours. The expression "nine-to-five" means practically nothing in a restaurant. With this kind of flexibility built in, it is often possible to find a schedule that fits in with other personal needs, such as being the primary care provider for a young family.

Catering houses may be an ideal answer, offering a young parent the chance to pick the days to work from among the various parties that the establishment has booked. Bakeshops often have early morning hours that might exactly suit the needs of a parent who has agreed to take over child care in the afternoons, when the children come home from school. Delicatessens and gourmet take-out shops may have openings for someone who can come in for one or two days a week to prepare a supply of salads and carry-out entrées. Restaurants may be willing to purchase cakes and other pastries prepared at home by a talented baker who would rather have most of his or her time free to pursue a career as a novelist. As you can see, the clock is seldom a barrier if you have the skill, the ingenuity, and the drive to find a rewarding job in this field.

Options for Women, Minorities, and the Disabled

Old-fashioned stereotypes sometimes stand between women and the highest positions in the field, even though a woman is just as capable as a man of working under pressure, in hot kitchens, lifting heavy pots, and standing on her feet for hours on end. Kitchens have not always been quick to embrace equality of the sexes. There is still a tendency to relegate women to the pantry, where they make salads all day, or to the bakeshop, where they produce cakes and pies. And, it must be said right here that there is absolutely nothing wrong with these jobs. If they are satisfying, pay well enough to make you happy, and leave you with enough energy at the end of the day to enjoy the rest of your life, then enjoy your choice and follow your career path with pride.

However, if you have your eye on administrative positions or the more glamorous jobs on the hot line, you should know that a woman is still more likely to meet with resistance than a man, unless she is working in a very special organization. Still, changes are happening, and there has never been a better time for women to enter this field. More and more fine restaurants have women heading their kitchen staffs as a whole new generation of chefs is coming into its own. Respect for the work that women are able to do in this field is coming, and the reins of tradition are loosening more each day as talented women of all ages and in all areas are being heard from.

If women have a hard time getting out of the bakeshop and the pantry, the same is true for minority workers. Their work as prep cook or pot washer has become such an entrenched part of the image of kitchen work that it has taken some special effort for minorities to move into the spotlight. There is no room for racial or gender bias in an industry that will go begging for skilled workers in the very near future. One has only to glance through a current food magazine to see a parade of new faces and cuisines with a decidedly global look.

People who are physically challenged are also more likely than ever before to find themselves able to work in this field. At first, the notion of a chef who can't see or who can't hear or who can't stand up at the stove may sound impossible. But, with each year, new equipment and better kitchen design make it possible for anyone willing to work hard to take part in this industry. And, as our society changes, the demands made on this industry change as well. Creative thinking, flexible attitudes, and a willingness to try have made it possible for Nell LaBarge, a graduate of the Culinary Institute of America, for example, to continue to work in the field she loves despite being wheelchair bound.

CHAPTER TWO

The Traditions of the Brigade

I n the previous chapter, most of the references to work in this field centered on the more traditional jobs in restaurants of hotel kitchens. There are plenty of other paths to take, but for now, let's focus on the more traveled route. After all, gourmets seem to find their happiest hours are spent dining in fine restaurants. Why shouldn't they also look for satisfaction on the job in the kitchens of those restaurants?

As you will see, the range of work experiences that you could have in the culinary field is limited only by your stamina and your personal interest. You may find that your personality and lifestyle are best complemented by work in an institutional feeding operation, such as college food service, where the hours are predictable; holidays and weekends could be free for you to spend with your family. Or you may crave the excitement and glamour of a white tablecloth restaurant enough to sacrifice a normal working schedule and much of the free time that everyone else in the world seems free to enjoy—except the chef.

As you continue on through your career, you will often feel a certain amount of conflict: should you take a job in a kitchen where you can earn a lot of money, or should you work in an operation where the pay is less impressive, but where you feel you can learn more? Choosing a new job, deciding when and for what reasons you will move from one job to the next—these are all quite personal decisions. But it is difficult to go too far wrong if you have developed your own career path thoughtfully. Chiseling that path, the one that is custom designed for you alone, is your responsibility. No one can do that for you. Learning what some of your options are is the purpose of this book, and the first step is to understand what actually goes on in a restaurant's kitchen.

When you look over a menu, you might find yourself wondering how on earth the restaurant manages to prepare so many different items. You probably know from personal experience how hard it is to prepare the five or six dishes that compose a meal and have them all finished and hot at the appropriate time. This is true whether you are working solo or you have a helper or two to take care of the scullery work, setting the table, and peeling the onions. Multiplying the work that goes into preparing one dinner with a preordained menu and no variations might make the work that goes on in a restaurant kitchen seem impossible to imagine. Are there simply several more people in the professional kitchen than you have in your own?

There may not be a whole battalion of chefs and cooks in the back of the restaurant, frantically scurrying around to prepare whatever guests order. The reason that modern restaurants are able to perform their feats of service is directly related to an organizational structure, first suggested by Escoffier, known as the brigade system. What it means is that each person has a defined scope of responsibility and designated tasks to perform. For instance, one person is in charge of preparing all the vegetables for every plate. Someone prepares just the sautéed dishes. The system has a special pecking order.

This organization wasn't always in place. In old-time kitchens, there were no exact job descriptions. When it was time to prepare a meal, whoever was free would start to work on it, assembling all of the various components as quickly as possible. You can imagine that this might be a little inefficient, and it was. The brigade system used today is a much better strategy. The hierarchy of the kitchen is outlined below, beginning with the administrative positions and then moving on through the rest of the kitchen.

Master Chef

This is the highest accolade the American Culinary Federation can confer on a chef. There are strict regulations that stipulate who will be accepted as a candidate for the examination. Those who qualify have spent a certain number of years working in professional kitchens and have already achieved the status of certified executive chef. In addition, they have accumulated a certain number of hours of continuing education and competed in recognized food shows. This is all kept track of through a system of points.

Once the necessary number of points are reached and other requirements are satisfied, the candidate undergoes a grueling examination, administered and scored by other master chefs and accepted professionals in related subject areas, such as nutrition and sanitation. It is important to demonstrate exceptional skill in different competencies, including all basic cooking methods, baking, presentation of foods, preparation of cold foods, and design of menus and restaurant facilities. The examination takes place over a number of days. The hours are cruel, and the pressure is intense. There are few master chefs in the world today. It is one of the highest honors one can achieve in this field.

Dave Megenis, a Certified Master Chef, said that it was without doubt one of the most difficult and challenging things he ever undertook, but "when you have finally made it through to the final dinner, your spirit soars knowing that you have achieved one of the highest accolades of our profession. You have to put a lot on the line, emotionally, financially, spiritually, and physically, to take this examination. Just meeting the guidelines is a big challenge. It is an honor to be able to write 'CMC' after my name."

Executive Chef

The executive chef is in charge of a large kitchen, sometimes even a chain of kitchens. This title should not be applied indiscriminately; specific standards must be met. In order to truly deserve the title of executive chef, the chef must have either a diploma or certificate granted by a school qualified to confer the title. The certificate is awarded to an individual based upon his or her years of experience and quality of work, in addition to formal education. If you see the letters CEC following someone's name, that person has been certified by the American Culinary Federation as a Certified Executive Chef."

The responsibilities of the executive chef are varied. This individual must oversee the operation of the entire kitchen with ultimate responsibility for the food and service offered by an establishment. It is this person's job to develop and maintain standards for the preparation and service of food. Menu development, recipe testing, training, and management of all aspects of the kitchen's operation are among the most important duties of the executive chef. Additional responsibilities, such as purchasing, costing, inventory, and other administrative chores, are also likely to be part of the work of the executive chef. In fact, it is common to hear executive chefs lament the amount of paperwork they are required to do and how little time they actually spend cooking.

Chef de Cuisine

A chef who has one or more professional cooks working for him or her is properly known as either the head chef or *chef de cuisine*. The latter term translates from French as "chef of all cuisine." As you will see from our discussion of the various jobs performed in the kitchen, many of the commonly used terms are French. Most professional cooks and chefs can use this terminology without batting an eye. The influence of France on all types of cooking is undeniable, and one of the lingering traces of French tradition is the use of French cooking terms even in English-speaking kitchens.

The head chef has numerous responsibilities, many of them quite similar to those of the executive chef. The head chef is the chief authority in the kitchen during all hours of operation. In an establishment that is not large enough to justify both an executive chef and a head chef, the jobs of both are handled by one person.

Sous-Chef

The person who is second in command in the kitchen is known as the *sous-chef*, or, as it translates, the "under chef." This is an administrative position, as is the position of the executive chef. The sous-chef usually is involved in actual food preparation, as well as having a hand in such duties as preparing work schedules, training new employees, preparing inventories, and assisting with purchasing. As you can see, rising through the ranks in the kitchen often involves becoming familiar with the business end of a restaurant. In today's world, that usually means becoming familiar with the use of a variety of software programs and computer applications.

There are a number of other positions in the restaurant, known collectively as line-cook positions. Another way to categorize this group of job descriptions is *chefs de parties*. These are the cooks responsible for preparing the menu items. This is where the professional kitchen's ability to prepare numerous dishes with speed and efficiency comes into clearer focus. By dividing the responsibilities of preparing menu items along a clear line, it is possible to streamline work so much that foods can be prepared quickly and efficiently, even if the actual kitchen staff seems quite small.

These jobs, or stations, as they are also known, constitute the second tier of workers in the brigade system. In this brief outline of the position titles and duties, the kitchen is divided into three distinct areas: the *hot line*, where all hot foods are prepared; the *cold line*, where salads, cold hors d'oeuvres, and appetizers, pâtés, terrines, and other cold items are prepared; and the *bakeshop*.

The Hot Line

The hot line is the area of the kitchen where foods are prepared for service. There are a number of stations on any hot line, but, as we will see, the needs of the kitchen and the size of the staff usually will determine how many of the stations are combined into one. For example, a small kitchen might have only two people actually cooking. This probably means that one person takes care of all the sautéed, grilled, and broiled items, while the other person prepares the vegetables as well as any cold dishes and desserts on the menu.

The two major positions on the hot line include the sauté cook and the grill cook. Other positions are equally important, but they tend to serve as supporting roles to these starring spots. We will look carefully at the work done by these two major stations, and follow them with a general discussion of additional work on the hot line.

Sauté Cook

The sauté cook, or *saucier*, as this person may also be known, is often considered the next in line to either the sous-chef, if there is one, or the head chef. This position is achieved only after spending a sufficient amount of time learning and practicing the craft of cooking.

The responsibilities for this spot on the hot line include the preparation of all dishes that are sautéed, including appetizers and entrées, the sauces to accompany these foods (hence the term *saucier* or "sauce chef"), any appropriate garnishes, from chopped parsley to puff pastry *fleurons*, and any *mise en place* necessary to accomplish the work of this station.

Mise en place is the professional cook's blanket term to describe any and all tools and ingredients that must be within arm's reach, prepared and ready for the chef to use for the actual preparation of meals during the service period (the hours that a restaurant is open and serving the public). For the sauté cook, *mise en place* will normally include an assembly of items such as chopped garlic, shallots, and perhaps ginger, salt and pepper, clarified butter, prepared sauces, wines, lemon juice, chopped fresh herbs, chopped fresh tomato, and whatever special items are dictated by the requirements of the menu. Tools such as pans, spoons, tongs, and cleaning supplies (wiping and sanitizing cloths), and a good supply of dry towels must also be within arm's reach.

The preparation of sauces normally requires the greatest sensitivity and talent. Some sauces are prepared in large batches in advance. These sauces are sometimes called grand sauces or mother sauces. From the grand sauces, it is easy to prepare smaller batches of sauces that are specially flavored and garnished for a single menu item. For example, the basic brown sauce, known as *fond de veau* or *jus de veau*, may be flavored with fortified wines such as Madeira, port, Marsala, or burgundy to create a "small sauce." Fresh herbs, diced or julienned meats, mushrooms, or other garnishes are added to create such special sauces as chasseur, *forestière*, or champignon. These few examples are just the tip of the iceberg, and it is part of the *saucier*'s skill to know several small sauces that can be prepared from *fond de veau* and other grand sauces, including velouté, béchamel, and tomato sauce.

Contemporary cooking styles have increased the number of sauces with which the sauté cook must be familiar. Some of these sauces cannot be prepared in advance, such as beurre blanc and sabayon, fragile sauces that are foams created *à la minute* based on the flavorful drippings released by sautéed foods. Other new items that are becoming standard fare on many menus include coulis (puree) of vegetables, light broth-based sauces, and a variety of salsas, relishes, marmalades, and chutneys. The skilled sauté cook needs to keep up-to-date with innovations in cooking styles so that the featured menu items and specials will attract interest among the guests.

The primary requirements for success at this glamorous but demanding position are organizational skills, split-second timing, the ability to keep a number of different tasks in mind at the same time, stamina, and grace under pressure. During a busy Saturday night, there probably will be orders for several tables in front of you at once. Each one needs to be attended to in the proper sequence, so that each table is completed in synchronization with other dishes from other stations, plated, and sent out of the kitchen all at the same time.

To further complicate matters, it is not always a simple matter of "first come, first serve." The waiter may come back to tell you that table thirty-six is lingering over their salads and won't be ready for about another fifteen minutes. This can present a problem; most kitchens use a fairly standard set of assumptions about when to prepare hot foods. When the guests change the pattern midstream, it is important that the sauté chef be able to adapt quickly so that the food doesn't become dry, overcooked, or inedible while it sits and waits for the guests to be ready.

Grill Cook

The French term for this station is *grillardin*, but unlike *saucier*, this term is not widely used in English-speaking kitchens. This position, along with the sauté station, is the most prestigious on the hot line. Today's guest is usually more sophisticated about food choices. Grilled and broiled foods have grown enormously in popularity for several reasons. Grilled foods have a special, bold flavor that many people find appealing. In addition, this cooking technique is generally regarded as a healthy way to cook foods deliciously without adding fats and oils during cooking.

Adventurous cooks are grilling more and more types of foods, up to and including breads, pizzas, and even fruits.

Just as the sauté cook is responsible for the preparation of any sauces, garnishes, and *mise en place* necessary for the work that must be done during a service period, so, too, is the grill cook. Some of the items may be identical to those required by the sauté cook, while others are uniquely suited to the demands of this particular station. The grill cook will probably use some of the same basic sauces, such as *fond de veau*, tomato sauce, or hollandaise. In addition, he or she will need to prepare compound butters, flavored oils, marinades, glazes, barbecue sauces, and other items used to give additional flavor to foods as they grill. The *mise en place* will typically include oil to lubricate both the foods being cooked and the rods of the grill, in addition to all of the prepared sauces. Chopped fresh herbs, tomatoes, and other items should be prepared as needed, according to the menu for the day. Brushes to apply glazes and marinades, a scraper or wire brush to clean the grills, sizzler platters, and other small tools, along with cleaning supplies, must also be gathered.

Most of the same qualities and abilities necessary for the sauté cook also apply to this station. It is just as nerve-wracking a position, and just as demanding when it comes to organizational skills. At any given time, it is likely that you might have a few appetizers "working" on the grill, several entrées, and one or two special items that you are called upon to prepare for other stations, such as the quickly charred red endive that will be used to garnish a sautéed dish, or grilled peppers that will be served room temperature in a vinaigrette with marinated goat cheese as an appetizer produced by the pantry station. In addition, the grill cook often is called upon to prepare any roasted items, such as roasted chicken or rack of lamb. It can be confusing to have to keep track of food on the grill, where it is out in the open, at the same time that you are preparing foods in the oven, where they are all too easy to forget.

One of the most challenging aspects of this station is determining the exact second that a piece of meat or fish is properly cooked. This is crucial for the sauté station as well, but it seems to be magnified in this spot because of the number of steaks, burgers, and chops that are requested at a very specific range of doneness, from "blue" to well-done. If a table orders two steaks, one hamburger, and a piece of swordfish from the grill, it is the grill cook's job to properly manipulate these foods so that one steak is cooked to rare, the other to medium well, the burger to medium rare, and the fish just to the exact point at which it is cooked through while still remaining moist. And each dish must finish cooking at the exact same time. This is no easy feat, although cooks employ some special strategies to make the job a little easier. The biggest issue is identifying that a steak is medium rare without cutting it open. This skill comes only through plenty of practice, as any talented grill cook will tell you right away. You have to rely on a built-in sense of about how long an item takes to get to a particular doneness, and also an intimate awareness of how a medium-rare steak feels to the touch as opposed to a steak that is cooked medium well. Each type of food has its own special characteristics, and it does take skill, as well as experience, to develop the deft hand and fine-tuned accuracy that make a great grill cook.

Other Positions

Obviously, no one starts at the top of the heap at the grill or sauté station. There are dues to pay and tricks to learn before you can call yourself a professional who is truly ready for such highly specialized work. But, along the way, there are plenty of other spots that offer distinct challenges as well as the opportunity to continue to hone your craft as you become more and more adept at a variety of aspects of this work. In this section we will look at a number of these spots and their basic duties.

Fish Cook

The fish cook, in a large kitchen, would be on the same basic line in an organizational flow chart as the sauté cook and the grill cook. In most operations, the duties of the fish cook are essentially the same as those of a sauté cook, with the exception that the fish cook's only responsibility is the preparation of all fish-based appetizers and entrées served hot. This includes, as you might expect, any sauces and garnishes necessary as well as the appropriate *mise en place*. Very often, however, the duties of the fish cook are distributed among other stations. The grill cook prepares all grilled and broiled seafood items, the sauté cook does the same for any sautéed appetizers or entrées. Any fish items that are deep-fried are prepared by whoever prepares other deep-fried menu selections.

As more and more guests turn to fish and seafood as healthy, delicious alternatives to red and white meats, seafood is becoming increasingly diverse, with new varieties that were hardly ever heard of even a few years ago. Familiar types of fish have become less readily available as demand has begun to outstrip supply in some instances. Aquaculture and fish farming have made some popular varieties such as trout, salmon, mussels, and oysters more consistently available, but other fish such as sea bass, striped bass, and red snapper have become more difficult to secure. This shortage has caused increased interest in a number of fish that used to be known as "trash fish." This term was never meant as a description of their flavor. Several of these so-called trash fish have a wonderful, delicate taste.

Because there are so many new types of seafood, cooks must be able to work with a number of different fish with skill and ease. This is not an easy task. The flesh of fish and shellfish is usually more delicate than that of beef, poultry, veal, pork, lamb, or game. It tends to cook very quickly when subjected to high temperatures. Overcooking is a serious concern. Timing and concentration are essential for anyone who wishes to cook fish properly. Fish is prepared by a wide variety of techniques, including grilling, sautéing, steaming, poaching, baking, and pan- and deep-frying. This means that the fish cook needs to be comfortable with moist and dry heat techniques and must be skilled at making the appropriate sauces to accompany fish prepared in such a wide array of fashions.

Pasta Cook

The pasta cook prepares a wide variety of appetizers, entrées, and side dishes. Dishes based on noodles and pasta are found in most cuisines throughout the entire world. The familiarity of most well-informed guests with a wide variety of these dishes makes appetizers and entrées based on pasta a natural choice for most menus. In addition to their undoubted popularity, pastas are usually quick and easy to prepare, highly adaptable to a number of different sauces and garnishes, and normally quite profitable for the restaurant since they can be less expensive to prepare than other items.

The pasta cook's work may be sufficiently heavy to require one person or more to get it all done, but very often it is subsumed into another station or combined with the vegetable station.

The Vegetable Station

The vegetable station is usually responsible for all phases of preparing vegetable dishes. In today's restaurant, vegetables are usually more important than in the past, when they were seen as simply a filler. No longer treated as an afterthought, the selection and variety of vegetables found in markets and on menus today is a far cry from the standard options of the past. As the work of the vegetable station has increased in importance, vegetables are being prepared in new ways not always considered appropriate to the vegetable kingdom, even a few years ago. Grilled vegetables such as fennel, radicchio, peppers, and plantains are as familiar today as the overworked (and usually overcooked) boiled carrots and peas, or butter-drenched green beans amandine.

In addition to vegetables, this station also encompasses the preparation and service of the various farinaceous dishes. Just as the quality and variety of vegetable dishes has increased in response to greater interest from guests, so have the range of other side dishes. Potatoes are still as popular as ever, but french fries and mashed potatoes are giving way to some new approaches that showcase the sweet earthy taste of the lowly tuber. Grains are growing more important on most menus, too. Barley, millet, polenta, and quinoa have joined ranks with rice to broaden the repertoire of grain dishes.

Quite often, the vegetable station includes the work of a position known in classically organized kitchens as the *entremetier*. This person would be responsible for the preparation of hot appetizers, soufflés, and possibly soups as well. Frequently, the person responsible for preparing these dishes is also in charge of preparing fried items, such as fritters, beignets, croquettes, and other deep-fried appetizers, side dishes, entrées, and occasionally even desserts. The fry cook, or *friteurier*, is a position that is often used as a stepping-stone to other jobs on the hot line. There is normally a significant amount of *mise en place* to be assembled, such as batters for tempura appetizers and entrées, breadings to be applied to meats, fish, poultry, and vegetables, and the base mixtures (known as *appareils*) for croquettes and fritters.

The Cold Line

In addition to the array of hot foods, numerous menu items are meant to be served chilled or room temperature. These items fall into the domain of the pantry, or the garde-manger area, as it is also often known. The fact that foods are served cold does not necessarily mean that the cook or chef will not apply heat to them. In fact, it is just as important for the cold line cooks to be familiar with the various techniques used for hot foods as it is for the sauté or grill cook.

The Butcher

Most professional kitchens do at least some of the work of cutting meats, fish, and poultry themselves. In an organization large enough to justify it, this work is often the responsibility of at least one person, or in very large operations, an entire butcher "shop" may be in operation. This station has some very important work to perform.

There aren't any "cheap" foods, and every item purchased by the kitchen should be handled with care and respect in order to get the greatest possible return from investing in the item, whether it is lettuce, olive oil, cheese, or coffee. This is even more important with meats, fish, and poultry. These are the items that can help to generate the greatest profit, as long as they are handled with skill and care.

The ability to trim away bones, gristle, silver skin, and other inedible parts of a whole fish or a leg of lamb without wasting any usable meat is crucial. In fact, many restaurants that do not have someone sufficiently trained to cut meats will rely on precut, preportioned meats to reduce the risk of loss through careless handling, even though precut items cost significantly more than whole fish or birds or larger cuts of meat that are trimmed and portioned to meet specific menu needs.

In additional to cleaning away the parts of the meat that will not be served to the guest, it is important to be able to make the meat or fish fit specific menu needs. This may mean butterflying meats, cutting pockets into chops, pounding cutlets of veal to paper thinness, preparing supremes of pheasant breast, glove-boning quail, or preparing medallions, tournedos, or chateaubriand.

The butcher's work is important to every station on the hot and cold lines that relies upon meats, fish, poultry, and game to prepare their menu items. Other items are normally prepared from the trim whenever possible. For example, bones and lean trim are often used to prepare stocks, broths, and sauces. Lean trim may also be used in forcemeats that form the basis of such dishes as pâtés, terrines, and galantines.

Many kitchens do not have enough staff to give one person sole responsibility for the preparation of meats and fish. This means that someone else will assume this work, or it may be divided between the other stations, so that the sauté cook is in charge of trimming, cutting, stuffing, and preparing the meats and fish used for that station, and the grill cook is similarly responsible for preparing his or her own *mise en place*.

Garde-Manger

The dishes that come under the umbrella term *garde-manger* are indeed extensive. The translation of *garde-manger* is "food keep," and it is usually concerned with foods that are prepared and preserved in some fashion so that they will last through extended storage. Normally, they are served cold, with appropriate sauces and garnishes.

Some typical items that fall under the control of the garde-manger chef include *pâté en croûte*, galantines, terrines, sausages, smoked and pickled meats, and a wide variety of cold hors d'oeuvres and canapés. Very often, cold foods form the focal point of elaborate food displays, so in addition to requiring some very specialized skills when it comes to working with food, an artistic eye and the ability to create visually impressive displays are also important.

Ice carvings, though they are most often thought of as serving no function other than decoration, were originally intended to keep foods cold throughout the life of the display. They frequently served as vessels to hold such items as shrimp or caviar. Working with ice is a special skill that requires a keen eye and some definite talent as a sculptor. Many people actually prefer the work of the cold station because, without the intense pressure of the hot line to prepare foods quickly so that the guest will be served in a timely fashion, there is a greater chance to express oneself artistically.

Pantry Cook

The pantry cook is normally responsible for all the work involved in preparing a variety of salads, including cleaning lettuces, cutting vegetable garnish, and preparing a variety of salad dressings. As you might expect, this position is frequently used to introduce a novice or new employee to the way that a particular kitchen operates. It should not be thought of as unimportant, however. A wonderful salad at the start of the meal is critical to the guest's enjoyment of the evening, just as a good cup of coffee enhances the end of the meal.

Salads are not the end of the story. Cold appetizers are usually plated (though not necessarily prepared from scratch) by the pantry cook. As an example, consider the platters of smoked fish or *charcuterie* plates featuring pâtés, cheeses, and other items crafted by the garde-manger chef. The item itself may have been produced elsewhere or purchased already prepared. However, the way it looks when it arrives in front of the guest is the craft of the pantry cook at work.

Another duty of the pantry cook is plating up and presenting desserts—including cakes, tortes, ice cream desserts, and fruit plates. Just as the pâté or sausage isn't usually prepared by the pantry cook, neither are many of the desserts. However, it is entirely likely that the pantry cook will make the custard sauce used to blanket a plate that will hold a sliver of a rich chocolate terrine or the raspberry puree used to decorate a creamy mousse.

Breakfast Cook

For many people, getting up before the sun to cook eggs and flapjacks might not seem the most exciting job in the world. But, the breakfast cook is often a very important cog in the wheel of a successful hotel or dining room operation. Today, a lot of work gets done at breakfast. Power lunches complete with martinis and red meat have given way to breakfasts with croissant, fresh juice, and omelets. The position of breakfast cook is far more prestigious than in the past. Bradley Ogden had a direct influence on this meal when he changed the face of breakfast at Compton Place in San Francisco. Today, it remains one of his "pets" at Lark Creek Inn, his own inn in Larkspur, California. He also featured it in his book, *Breakfast, Lunch, and Dinner*. Other talented chefs have also changed the way that breakfast is prepared and eaten throughout the country.

If there is any doubt about the regard a true professional cook has for breakfast cookery, remember this: the hundred or so pleats adorning the tall white hats worn by chefs are said to represent the number of ways that a real chef can prepare eggs. And, of course, eggs aren't the last word in breakfast any longer. Pancakes, waffles, and other dishes are equally important, as are some new twists on old favorites inspired by the ongoing passion for health and fitness.

The Bakeshop

It is undeniably true that a good chef must be well versed in all areas of the kitchen, including the bakeshop. An ability to work with a variety of pastry doughs, mousses, and other mixtures more commonly associated with the bakeshop indicates a chef with a serious commitment to excellence.

However, it is equally true that some people will find themselves more drawn to work in bakeshop than they are to the kitchen. There are a number of differences between life as a pastry chef and life as an executive or head chef. There is no difference, however, in the respect received by those who reach the upper levels in either branch of the culinary art.

Many operations are large enough to be able to support the work of a full-scale bakeshop or to afford the salary of a topnotch pastry chef. Hotels, resorts, and large catering houses and restaurants may have in-house bakeshops, but other restaurants will often buy at least some goods already prepared from independent bakeshops.

Within this discipline, there are usually two major divisions. Bakers prepare breads, simple cakes, and pies. Pastry chefs are the ones responsible for tortes, French pastries, petits fours, and other more elaborate and decorated pastries. Both jobs are equally challenging. Both the baker and the pastry chef are talented individuals who must be able to work with formulas carefully, adjusting at all times for slight differences in humidity, oven temperature, and other variables.

Bakers

Bakeshops are noted primarily for their production of muffins, quick breads, yeast breads, rolls, and simple desserts. It is work that demands skill, creativity, and the ability to produce large numbers of products quickly and efficiently.

Quick breads, muffins, and other simple batters are relatively easy to prepare, but a bakeshop can make or break its reputation on their quality. Since bakeshops are traditionally open early in the morning, people will get in the habit of stopping by for a bran muffin and coffee on the way to work—if your bran muffins are the best in town. And then, they will most likely remember to stop by on the way home for a loaf of bread for dinner or a pie for dessert.

Bakers must be able to scale (or measure) ingredients accurately, mix them properly, and bake them correctly. This is not a simple matter of following a formula, however. On any given day, the air may be more humid or the flour may be a little "harder" or "dryer" than the last batch. Consistency can only be assured by bakers who are skilled enough to see or feel the difference in a dough and make the correct adjustment.

Many large-scale bakeshops make use of machines to mix and shape doughs. This assures greater uniformity of production. The chain of command in a bakeshop is similar to the hierarchy of a kitchen. There is a head baker, an assistant baker, and then as many additional workers as necessary to meet the daily production quota.

The hours for a baker are rigorous, just as they are for most other people working in the culinary arts. Bakers, however, usually start work before the sun comes up and finish about the time the chefs who work dinner shift are coming in to work.

Some bakeshops do the work from start to finish; others purchase products that are partially prepared. One bakeshop will have its own "secret" formulas for breads, muffins, and cupcakes. Others will purchase frozen doughs and finish baking them. Of course, the level of expertise required from the workers will determine how well they are paid.

Many hotels and supermarkets, and even some fast-food chains that offer fresh-baked goods, will have to do at least some of the baking directly on the premises. While this is often nothing more complicated than adding the required amount of liquid to a prepared mix, it sometimes means making more complicated items, such as Danish pastries or doughnuts, that require filling, frosting, and glazing.

Pastry Chefs

Pastry shops are responsible for preparing the more elaborate baked items. These items include small French pastries, elaborate cakes, wedding cakes, candies, and other specialty items.

The work done in pastry shops is even more exacting than that done in a bakeshop. The creations produced require a certain sense of form, line, and balance. These are the creations that cause people to stop in their tracks.

Working with chocolate and sugar are among the special skills that pastry chefs must have. These talents take a great deal of time, training, patience, and practice to develop.

It is common for a trained chef to decide to move into this demanding and specialized field. Quite often, he or she will elect to continue training, either by attending a school dedicated to teaching this craft or by working closely with a respected pastry chef.

Just as there are certified executive chefs and certified master chefs, there are also certified master pastry chefs. This honor is bestowed on those people who complete the required, and rigorous, course of studies and examinations and gain the appropriate experience.

Food and Beverage Managers

In addition to careers that will have you in the kitchen working with food on a day-to-day basis, there are other avenues you can take. Many people find that, as their lives and interests change, they are ready to move from a position in the kitchen, no matter how responsible, to management of an operation.

The position of food and beverage manager (or F & B, as it is often known) is sought by many in the culinary field. Prospective F & B managers make careful decisions regarding the type of education they will receive and where they will receive it. The management of an operation is a job that requires many talents. In the past, there was a great perceived difference between chefs and F & B managers. In fact, the best F & B managers are those who share the chef's practical knowledge of what it takes to create fine cuisine. As more and more people move from the kitchen into management, the overall operation of a hotel almost invariably benefits.

The chef turned manager can offer many skills that someone trained solely in business management cannot. Business managers very often spend some time looking at how a restaurant operation affects a larger business, but without a good feeling for what is actually possible in a particular kitchen, or in a certain type of dining room, it's difficult for managers to make sound, practical decisions.

CHAPTER THREE

Working in Restaurants and Institutions

There is no single, typical restaurant or hotel that will provide a perfectly accurate picture of this business. Each day brings new challenges and new opportunities. This might be the day that the meat delivery arrives and you find that, instead of precut veal scallopini, you have received a whole leg of veal. And, so, this might be the day that you learn to break down a leg of veal, cut, and pound the scallopini yourself. Or this might be one of the slowest nights of the year, when you spend the entire evening meal service period cleaning out the walk-in, scouring the cutting boards, and putting spices into alphabetical order. However, for the sake of argument, let us imagine that there is a restaurant, somewhere in the world, where life actually follows a specific plan. And let's follow several kitchen workers through an ordinary day. In this restaurant, all of the foods, with a very few exceptions, are prepared from scratch. Dinner is served six days a week, and on Sunday, there is a brunch.

The à la Carte Kitchen

An à la carte kitchen is one where a menu is offered with several different dishes, all priced separately. The guest selects from those dishes to create a meal of several courses, or just a few, as he or she wishes. In fact, the term *à la carte* translates into English as "from the menu."

The staff in this kitchen must be able to prepare, at any given moment, a great variety of dishes, in the proper sequence, and grouped so that they are ready to be served at the correct time. The typical day we will follow includes the work done by a number of different cooks, bakers, and assistants. All are required to achieve one single aim: having the entire kitchen in a state of such total readiness that the line cooks can work without stopping once or leaving their stations from the time that the first order goes out to the time that the final dessert is served, wasting as little of any resource as possible.

As you can imagine, such a demanding task can only be accomplished if everyone organizes their work properly and completes tasks efficiently. This is all part of what sets a professional apart from everyone else. Professionals know the importance of getting all of the backup work done, taking as much care each step of the way as they would lavish on putting the final touches on an entrée.

The Baker

The first to arrive will be the baker. In this kitchen, the baker also fills the role of pastry chef. It may well be three or four in the morning when the baker unlocks the kitchen door, flips on the lights, and gets ready to start weighing out ingredients to make the three or four varieties of yeast bread that need to be made that day. Once all the ingredients are properly scaled, the baker will mix the doughs, using large mixers fitted with dough hooks. Each dough has a specific texture, appearance, and feel that tell the baker when it is properly mixed and kneaded.

Now, the doughs are placed in bowls, covered with clean cloths, and left to rise in a place that is warm and draft free. While they undergo the first rise, the baker turns his or her attention to some of the special desserts to be prepared. Usually, there are several different components, and each one must be prepared in a logical sequence. Perhaps today the baker is making sponge cakes (known as genoise) to form the basis of several other desserts. Again, all of the ingredients are carefully weighed out. A professional baker will always weigh ingredients when possible so that the formula is prepared as accurately as possible. There are always some subtle adjustments that may be required to accommodate a day that is really humid or a batch of butter that has more liquid than the one before. However, the baker's formulas are usually as precise and accurate as they can be, and it is important to follow them carefully for the most consistent results.

After weighing out the ingredients, the pans are assembled and prepared, and the ovens are lit. Once the fragile batter is properly mixed, it is again weighed, placed in the pans, and then immediately put into the oven so that as little volume as possible will be lost. As you can see, it is important to have an organized approach to work so that everything is ready at the right time. After the cakes are in the oven, it is time to turn attention to the other dessert items featured on the menu.

The crust for fruit tarts must be mixed and then allowed time to rest in the refrigerator before it is rolled out and gently fitted into tart pans. So that might be the next task. Or perhaps the chef has asked for puff pastry to be prepared for use in a variety of appetizers. This rich dough is made over the course of two days so that it never becomes too warm. The baker may prepare the dough today and give the dough the first of a sequence of folding and rolling that results in a flaky pastry that increases its volume by three times when it bakes.

Then, once the cakes are removed from the oven, it will most likely be time to turn back to the bread dough. If the dough is properly risen, it will be punched down, turned out onto a work surface, shaped into rounds, and allowed to rest and rise again. This is known as "bench proofing," and it allows the dough to relax enough to be easily coaxed into the various shapes it will be baked in—loaves, rolls, rings, and braids. Once the dough is shaped and placed onto the correct type of baking pan, it is allowed to rise a final time. Depending upon the type of dough, this might be done in a proof box that will bathe the dough in steam.

As the dough undergoes its final rise, the baker will probably begin to assemble ingredients for the variety of frostings, fillings, and glazes used to decorate the tarts, tortes, and other pastries that fall under the baker's job description. Perhaps he or she will begin the preliminary work on decorating a wedding cake or piping a delicate decoration on petits fours to be served at high tea. The cheesecakes prepared yesterday might be topped with fruits, or the chocolate mousse cake might need to be filled and decorated.

Some of this specialized work might have to be done in a separate area of the bakeshop, away from the heat of the ovens. Maybe the crepes for a banquet must be prepared, or perhaps the muffins and quick breads to fill the baskets for Sunday brunch are on the list for today.

The final work of the day, once the breads are baked and removed from the oven, and the tart shells are baked and gently stored until the next day when they will be filled, is to prepare a number of hand-dipped chocolates that are served at the end of the meal, a *mignardise* to sweeten the bill. Working with chocolate is the most interesting and delicate type of work that the pastry chef will undertake. The chocolate is gently tempered, coaxed to the exact temperature at which it coats evenly and smoothly, drying to a hard glossy shine. The filling is a rich ganache made from chocolate and cream, flavored with special liqueurs.

Once these baked goods and confections are stored and ready for service, the baker finishes the day by scrubbing down all the work surfaces, tools, and equipment in the work area. Most likely he or she will also be found sweeping the floor and removing the garbage, unless there is a pot washer around to do this last chore. When the baker is done and ready to toss the morning's apron into the laundry bag, the pantry cook is just arriving. It is around 11 A.M.

The Pantry and Prep Cooks

The next to arrive are a couple of cooks who are just starting their careers. They have pantry and preparation (prep) positions. The pantry cook is responsible for preparing all of the salads, including the dressings, as well as the garnishes for a variety of cold appetizers. The prep cook usually has a variety of jobs that will change from day to day. The morning is usually devoted to accomplishing a number of tasks written down by the line cooks and the chef at the end of the evening's shift the night before.

First, the pantry cook checks the salads and dressings that are left from the night before. Any that have outlived their best quality are disposed of. Next, he or she needs to decide how to organize the work to accomplish. There are different factors that will enter into the prioritization of work. What takes the longest? Which items need time to marinate? Which flavors will be best if they are allowed plenty of time to mature? Which foods should be handled as little as possible so that they are as fresh, crisp, and flavorful as possible when they are served to the guest?

Knowing all of these considerations are important, the pantry cook decides to start by preparing a variety of relishes and condiments so that their flavors can develop over several hours. Next come some salad dressings. Then croutons and rusks are seasoned and baked so that they will have time to cool before they are needed. If the pantry cook is responsible for preparing items such as grilled peppers, marinated vegetables, and meats and fish used in a variety of salads, they must be properly cooked in plenty of time to assure that they are ready when needed. Finally, the more fragile lettuces and greens are rinsed carefully and cut or torn to the right size.

While all of this is going on, the prep cook is hard at work completing a variety of tasks. The prep cook must also learn to organize the jobs to be done into a smooth schedule, completing the work properly and in plenty of time. First, long-simmering stocks and broths are probably started. There is usually a great deal to gather before the stock is put on the stove. The bones need to be rinsed and browned, *mirepoix* (a combination of onions, carrots, celery, and other vegetables) has to be peeled and chopped. Seasoning ingredients including *sachet d'épices* (a small bag of spices and dried herbs) and bouquet garni (a bundle of fresh herbs and aromatic vegetables) have to be put together. Then, the cooking process needs to be carefully monitored until the correct cooking speed is reached. Now, the prep cook can turn most of his or her attention elsewhere, returning occasionally to skim the surface and then check to be sure that the stock is "working" at just the right speed—not too hot, not too cold, not too fast, not too slow.

Next, the prep cook may need to prepare the vegetables for a variety of soups and other basic sauces. Garlic and shallots must be peeled and minced, or perhaps roasted and pureed. Pine nuts that will be sprinkled over an appetizer must be toasted carefully and cooled. Several types of pasta may be cooked until still slightly underdone, rinsed, coated with oil, and then carefully stored and wrapped to be ready for the evening's dinner service. Closer to the time when the chefs and cooks are actually ready to start preparing meals, fresh herbs may be rinsed and chopped. Other ingredients that they may need, such as clarified butter, bread crumbs, and grated cheese will also have to be fit into the day's work so that a complete *mise en place* is ready for the entire kitchen. There is a great deal of satisfaction in this job, and a little less pressure than the stress faced by the sauté cook, who may have to keep the dinner orders from several different tables in mind at once. Virtually everyone who works in a kitchen has spent time peeling carrots and scrubbing mussel shells.

Now that the list is completely checked off, it is time to strain the stocks, cool them in an ice water bath, put them into storage containers, write out labels and dates, and stow them away in the reach-ins and walk-ins that hold all the kitchen's perishable goods. Cutting boards and work tables are wiped down, and the pantry cook ends the day by cleaning and honing the used knives before putting them into his or her knife kit.

The Line Cooks and the Sous-Chef

A few hours after the pantry and prep cooks arrive, the line cooks and sous-chef are ready to start. There is always a great deal to accomplish. The training and skills that these cooks bring to their work set a good restaurant apart from a mediocre one. The first step is getting organized. Each person will check the *mise en place* carefully to see what is missing, or what they may need to have more of so that they don't run out in the middle of service.

To get an idea of how much they may need for that evening, they will all want to know how many are "on the book," or, to translate, how many reservations the restaurant has that night. Of course, most restaurants do accept a certain number of walk-ins in addition to those with reservations. This means that the cooks must use judgment and past experience, coupled with a little educated guessing, to decide how much to prepare. It is not a good idea to have to stop in the middle of dinner service to fillet and slice a salmon. On the other hand, it is very bad practice to get so much food ready that it spoils long before it can be served. Food that is thrown away is nothing but a drain on the profits of a restaurant. And even if you don't own the restaurant, you have to be concerned about waste. This is a volatile business, and unless a restaurant consistently turns a profit, the owners will one day find that they cannot open the door, and then you are out of a job.

Let's follow a sauté cook through her rounds as she gets ready for a busy Saturday night. Most likely, she thought about what she would need to do as she traveled to work. Perhaps she already has a partial list organized before she evens sets foot in the door.

After an inspection of the items that are already prepared, this list is probably going to be refined. The sous-chef or the head chef may have decided to include a new appetizer to be featured on tonight's special list that calls for her to make fresh tortellini with a goat cheese and wild mushroom stuffing. The dough has to be mixed and given time to rest before it can be rolled out, cut, filled, and folded. This work has to be properly positioned in the sequence of other jobs.

In this restaurant, there is no separate butcher. Very often, the sous-chef will do this work herself. First, she will do all the beef items. Once they are properly trimmed, portioned, wrapped, and stowed in the correct refrigerator (or "box" as the cooks usually call them), and the cutting boards are properly scrubbed and sanitized, the next task will be chickens. The same sequence is repeated until every steak, chop, paillard, scallopini, supreme, fillet, and cutlet is finished. Or the individual line cooks may take the responsibility for a few items that are featured from their stations. The grill cook might make certain that the tuna is cut into steaks, and the sauté cook might be responsible for seasoning and tying the venison loin.

There are usually sauces, soups, and other things to make that take longer to prepare than other items. Some of these were prepared early in the afternoon so they will finish cooking far advance of service, to give them plenty of time to cool down for storage. *Jus de veau*, a basic brown sauce, is one such preparation. Pureed soups, bisques, consommés, and tomato sauce are other examples. Some items may take a long time to cook but aren't intended as something to prepare in advance and then hold. Casseroled potatoes should be put into the oven at the right time to be certain that they finish cooking as close as possible to the time at which they are supposed to be served for the best flavor and texture.

As the evening draws close, someone will prepare "family meal." This dinner is a break for the kitchen and dining room staff. If the preparation for the night has gone well so far, everyone will have a chance to take a break, sit down, and eat together. This is a good time to let the tensions lift for a little while and to get refreshed for the hectic night.

Dinner Service

Back on the line, the cooks check their stations to be certain that they have all the garnishes, seasoning, wines, lemon juice, butter, herbs, oils, brushes, spoons, tongs, pans, bowls, plates, and cleaning supplies they need for the next several hours. No one wants to have to leave his or her spot.

The sauté cook checks the ovens to be sure they are lit and at the right temperatures. The broiler cook makes certain a pot of water is ready to steam vegetables and another is set up to reheat pasta. The pantry cook has a store of plates in a reach-in box, keeping them cool so that the salads will stay at the perfect temperature.

And now it begins.

The first few tables of the night place their orders, and waiters bring them back to the kitchen. If the sous-chef is there, he or she will probably be the one who calls out the orders to the rest of the kitchen and will keep track of the sequence in which things are being prepared. The sequence of courses follows an established routine, with relatively little variation. Each restaurant will allow an average amount of time for the guests to enjoy a particular course.

One table requests two special salads, grilled mushrooms, and a soup to start the meal. Next, three of the party will have soup, and the fourth will have nothing. Finally, two people have requested entrées from the regular menu, one has ordered from the special list, and the fourth has requested one of the hot appetizers instead of an entrée. This sounds confusing, and it could be. However, the sous-chef knows which courses contain which foods and will be certain that the hot foods get prepared (or "fired") in such a way that all of the dishes are finished and at the correct temperature just when they should be.

Sometimes a table will be in a rush to get finished so that they can make it to a movie or concert on time. Other guests will prefer to linger over a leisurely meal, sipping wine and taking plenty of time between courses. The wait staff must keep the sous-chef informed about the "personality" of the table, so that the usual pattern is modified to meet the special needs of individual guests.

This particular Saturday night is extremely busy but also incredibly smooth. The night gets busier and busier, reaching a crescendo at around 9:30 or 10:00. Then, things begin to slow down gradually, and finally, at around 11:00, the last soufflé has been served, the final truffle has arrived at the table of the last remaining guests, and the kitchen staff is carefully cooling, storing, wrapping, and labeling the food. They may be preparing lists to get ready for the next day. The sous-chef is probably talking to the dining room manager to find out what went over well and which dish was not moving and getting ready to prepare a purchasing list to replenish the kitchen's stores.

Back in the kitchen, the cleaning crew is hard at work. Stoves are scrubbed to within an inch of their lives, counters are cleaned and polished, and pots and pans are scoured. When the last sheet pan is stored, the final garbage pail removed and emptied, the last stretch of floor swept and mopped, it's time to turn out the lights and go home.

Institutions

Institutional feeding is an area that many people overlook when considering a career in the culinary arts. The word *institutional* may not have exactly the right connotation for them. Actually, however, working in institutional feeding can be every bit as challenging, creative, and rewarding as work in a white-tablecloth restaurant.

There are substantial advantages to working for institutions, such as hospitals and schools. Depending upon your own needs and those of your family, this field could be just right for you.

The first distinct advantage to working in institutional feeding is that, most often, your hours will be regular, and you probably will not have to work on weekends or holidays. School cafeterias, for instance, usually close during winter, spring, and summer breaks. Many people prefer a calm, reliable schedule to the hectic pace of restaurant work.

Secondly, institutions provide the opportunity to learn additional skills. For instance, you may be able to learn about purchasing for large organizations, which could eventually lead to an excellent position as steward or purchasing agent for a school, hospital, or other institution.

Finally, and this is the advantage that often catches the eye of many people, larger organizations can afford to offer their employees a very appealing benefits package. It may include such things as paid vacations, sick days, personal time, medical and dental insurance, life insurance, even profit sharing. These benefits are not always possible in smaller operations. If you have a family, simply stop to consider the cost of life and health insurance if you had to get it on your own.

In addition to the practical advantages, institutional feeding is far more exciting than you might at first think based on its unfortunate-sounding name. While hospitals, schools, nursing homes, and airlines may not have the same glamour factor that a three-star, white-tablecloth restaurant does, the fundamental work is the same: to provide good, fresh, wholesome food to guests, whoever those guests are and wherever you may find them.

Schools, Colleges, and Universities

Most schools have some sort of on-site cafeteria. Larger schools, colleges, and universities may have a variety of food service operations on campus, including a traditional cafeteria, a fast-food restaurant, a coffee shop, or other options.

Very often, a large organization that handles the food service operation of several schools will be in charge. In that case, the managers will have received training from the group. (The American Restaurant Association, or ARA, is one such organization that operates nationwide.)

The chef or chef/manager is responsible for developing menus or for implementing the menus that are developed by the company itself. Usually modifications are required, and there is the inevitable need to work with the students, who are the ultimate consumers of the food. They will have specific demands and requests, as well. The area of the country will play a part, as will the economic profile of the school.

In addition to overseeing the production of the menus, the chef will also be required to schedule the workers. The division of work in the kitchen for a school food service operation is much like it would be for any other kitchen. There will be breakfast cooks, pantry (salad) workers, and hot-line cooks who will prepare the food that is served on the cafeteria line. There may be a separate bakeshop as well that prepares a variety of items, including desserts.

Then, there are the dish room staff, the servers who plate up and serve the food on the line, and other maintenance and service staff. Very often, the less skilled jobs are filled by student workers.

Hospitals

Hospitals do not have a reputation for serving good or, in some cases, even palatable food. But this doesn't have to be the case.

In fact, many hospitals have begun to make drastic changes in the kinds of foods they prepare, making the menu options more appropriate and appealing to their patients.

While some patients still need bland foods, a person in traction doesn't need to worry that a few spices in the meat loaf will send him or her into a tailspin. The kitchen staff in a hospital will need to work closely with the dieticians and the physicians to make sure that each patient's needs are met. The foods prepared and served to patients are part of the total care that they are receiving, and food can have a strong impact on a patient's morale.

It is a curious phenomenon that institutions dedicated to healing people have such a notoriously poor reputation when it comes to feeding them. Part of the problem in the past may have been that decisions about food were left to dieticians. These trained professionals certainly know about what foods are best. However, they are seldom skilled at making those foods appealing to someone who may have very little else to look forward to over the course of the day.

Nursing Homes

As people age, they gradually lose their sense of hearing, their sense of sight. It is rare, however, for them to lose their sense of smell or their ability to taste and enjoy foods. If hospitals have endured countless jokes about how poor the food is while nursing homes have escaped notice, it's probably because few comedians have checked into a nursing home for an extended stay.

Dave Stewart, chef and food service director for Salem Foodservice Company, is truly enthusiastic about his work in a special retirement center in New Jersey. He hardly sees it as boring or lacking in opportunities to be creative. "In order to effectively meet the standards established to regulate health care for the elderly, it is imperative that the quality of life in any health care facility be comparable to that found in the 'real' world." What this translates into, for Dave Stewart and the residents of the facility he operates, might surprise people who haven't given this type of work much thought. He puts on wine and cheese parties for residents, offers pizzas and Chinese food, and provides a very special service that allows residents to hold parties and family reunions either in the facility or at an off-site location. This allows residents to entertain the way they would like to and helps them stay in touch with friends, family, and the community.

Lately, Dave has even begun investigating how he might introduce some new cooking styles. He is especially interested in being able to offer the residents healthy, nutritious, and contemporary cuisine. That is hardly the extent of his work, though it sounds like enough to keep ten people busy all day long. He also operates a meals-on-wheels service for nonresidents in the community. Obviously, there is a lot more to working in a nursing home or retirement center than many of us might have ever imagined.

A variety of physical ills can beset the elderly, and this certainly affects the kinds of foods they are able to eat. If they have no teeth, or only poorly and loosely fit dentures, foods that require a good firm bite may be out of the question. Their physical condition may call for a modification of their diet—for instance, controlling the amount of cholesterol or sodium in the food. Still, there is a great deal of opportunity to make sure that the food prepared and served to guests of nursing homes is wholesome, nutritious, and interesting. And, for some, this work offers a special kind of reward.

Armed Forces

A large number of people who have entered the food service industry in the private sector have done so after learning their skills in the armed forces. Mess halls aren't the only dining options, and it is more than possible to learn a great deal about food preparation, even food preparation of the highest caliber, in the armed forces.

The range of work for kitchen personnel in the armed forces is identical to that of a very large, very well-organized hotel chain. There are executive chefs, chefs, sous-chefs, line cooks, pantry cooks, and bakers.

Prisons

Another institutional option is in prisons. City, county, state, and federal prisons have to feed their inmates. They have a moral and legal responsibility to assure that inmates' physical needs for clothing, shelter, and food are supplied. They have an equal obligation to the taxpayers who finance penal institutions to try to keep their efforts within a specified budget.

The challenge for the director of the food service operation is to make sure that three wholesome meals are served each day. It is important to learn how to get and use surplus items available through government programs, how to buy in bulk, and how to produce large amounts of food quickly and efficiently. This type of work is not for everyone, but it can be a rewarding job for some.

Dave Shepard finds his work as director of food service for Dutchess County jails to be extremely satisfying and challenging. "It forces me to channel my creative energies into providing the best, most nutritious and wholesome meals I can, within a very restricted budget."

Contract Feeding

Many companies operate cafeterias for their employees, or they may contract with "lunch wagons" to come to the work site during coffee breaks and lunch hours for the convenience of their employees. They also find it more efficient to be able to keep their employees close to work during the day.

The size and general working philosophy of the company will determine how much or little they expect from a contract feeding service. Since the employees will be paying for their meals, the food must be appealing enough so they will elect to buy it, rather than bringing their own food or leaving work at lunchtime.

Lunch wagons are often owned by one person, who determines what kind of food to offer and how much of it to prepare. There is a definite profit potential for the operators of these wagons. The hours can be long, but the rewards are usually ample.

A number of regulations must be met in order to operate such a business, and it is very important that you understand all the laws governing this type of business. You will need permits, inspections, and perhaps special insurance. Make sure that you fully investigate all the requirements first.

Airlines

No food, with the possible exception of hospital food, has a worse reputation than that found on airplanes. And while this may be justified in some cases, it certainly isn't automatically true. Airlines are a business, and they need to remain competitive in order to attract business. People want good, hot food, whether they are on the ground or in the air. Consumers are demanding, and getting, better food on airplanes.

Food service operations, such as Marriott, that hold contracts to prepare airline food must perform what might sound like a miracle. Large quantities of food must be prepared, portioned, and packaged to fit into a specified amount of space, requiring no additional preparation apart from heating.

John Keglovicz admits to being more than a little daunted by the sheer volume of work and some of the very unusual problems that faced him when he started work as a chef developing menus for a major airline. The amount of food, the number of selections offered, the cramped quarters on the airlines, and the outlandish requests made by passengers and airline directors alike nearly sent him into sensory overload during the first few months of his employment. Now, however, he finds that it is like working out a special puzzle, or finding the perfect move to make in a chess game. His creativity and enthusiasm illustrate the possibilities open to those who are willing to consider institutional feeding as a career.

CHAPTER FOUR

Catering

A catered event may be over in just a few hours, but the time that goes into planning each and every detail is hard to even count up accurately. There is a different kind of tension involved with banquet cooking. Unlike an à la carte kitchen, where there is no telling how many people will be there or how many will order the chicken as opposed to the fish, the banquet chef has a fairly good idea of how many guests will be eating, exactly what they will eat, and what time the food will be served. But even with the most careful planning, the most minutely organized timetable, seldom does everything go off without a hitch. It is the ability of everyone involved to find a quick, smooth, and calm way out of trouble that keeps these special events afloat.

The banquet chef for a hotel is in charge of a very important area of the hotel's business. Many operations count on conventions, meetings, and special events such as weddings, bar mitzvahs, and receptions to generate a large part of their revenue. The banquet chef is crucial to the success or failure of this part of the operation. She or he must follow an entirely different cadence than an à la carte kitchen. The work begins far in advance of the event, and the skills required to bring a catered event off successfully are varied indeed.

The ability to carefully organize an incredible number of details cannot be overstated. You are in charge, and if you enjoy being on display, then this area could be the perfect direction for you. But, as you can see, you owe it to yourself to test the waters and test yourself. The physical and emotional demands of working in catering are great. You might be making canapés for three thousand people or preparing one hundred perfect sunny-side up eggs. Perhaps you will be responsible for making sure that there are enough tables for a buffet or enough champagne tulips to serve the intermezzo, or you might have to prepare or purchase and pick up an ice carving. It may be necessary to coordinate with the bakeshop to make sure that the roses on the wedding cake are the same color as the linens, which should be the same color as the bridesmaids' gowns. But, then, as great as the challenges are, so are the rewards and the satisfactions.

In a very large hotel, it is entirely possible that there may be several different events taking place on the same day. Dovetailing all the advance preparation, the actual cooking and service of the food, is a job that requires enormous reserves of concentration, endurance, and skill.

On-Premise Catering

When there are large parties or banquets to be produced by a kitchen, the banquet chef must be able to wear a great many hats. The banquet chef is responsible for developing a number of different menus that must then be adjusted to meet the special needs or requirements of the guests. The menu must be carefully priced so that the customers perceive the value they are getting and also so that the greatest possible amount of profit is generated from the event. It is generally easier to meet a desirable profit margin when you know in advance how many people will be dining, at exactly what time, and on exactly which evening. An à la carte restaurant chef does not have this luxury.

However, a large part of the work requires business and selling skills—the factors that make a good banquet chef into a great one. He or she will help the guest determine what sort of hors d'oeuvres would be appropriate for a reception. The chef may also be able to arrange various styles of buffets, knowing that what might be correct for a cocktail reception following an opening at the museum will not work for a wedding reception. The banquet chef must be able to present the foods in a graceful and appropriate fashion and decide how best to serve the food, whether by passing the items "butler" style or by arranging them on a display.

The menu must be determined in advance and be suitable to the occasion. If there will be hors d'oeuvres followed by a meal, the hors d'oeuvres should harmonize with the foods being served later. And they must be attractive enough to invite the guest to try them, without being so large or so heavy that guests won't enjoy the meal that follows.

A Wedding

To get a better idea of what would occur during a typical in-house catered affair, let's look at a typical party—in this case, a wedding reception at an inn. The entire affair is arranged by the inn's owners, Denise and Allan Katz.

A young couple, or just as likely the bride and her mother, arrive to discuss booking the hotel's dining room for the wedding reception. They may, or may not, have a firm date in mind. Denise will need to go over the times of the event, what hours they have in mind, and ask them a host of other questions. "Would you like to offer a full or limited bar? A disc jockey, house band, or small string ensemble? A flower service? A house photographer?"

Denise also offers them a special pricing package for the wedding party and other guests who will be arriving from a distance or who simply would prefer the convenience of staying in the hotel on the evening of the reception. Once the basic outline of the event has been established, Allan is there to discuss the menu.

People may come to caterers expecting to be guided by them. Others have very definite ideas of their own. Many banquet chefs will have prepared a number of different menus and determined the selling price for the banquet ahead of time. Allan finds that it is important to have at least half a dozen menus, all kept up-to-date with frequent revisions to incorporate seasonal items and other attractive and irresistible dishes. Then, as the clients have a chance to look over the written menus, there is usually a great deal of give and take as items are selected, sampled, and compared.

With the menu determined, hours established, and all other ancillary offerings (flowers, photography, and so forth) factored in, Denise can calculate the selling price for a reception. By keeping her past records on file on computer and constantly updating information about food costs, labor costs, unforeseen circumstances, and other data that might be used in the future, she has managed to build up an enviable catalog of information. The care and attention she puts into keeping accurate and complete records has made each new event easier than the ones before. The major costs that make up the final bill include:

- Additional kitchen or wait staff prior to and on the day of the event

- Any cost for the rental or laundering of equipment, china, linen, glassware

- Flowers

- Music

- The wedding cake

- Any and all special requests

Special requests can be fruit baskets or cookies in every guest's room, favors for every guest, an additional vegetarian entrée, or special candles.

Early on in the discussions with the client, the banquet manager will be able to offer very accurate estimates. As the date of the event grows closer, and the number of guests starts to become more settled, he or she may review all the calculations once more, especially if there have been many changes and modifications along the way. Denise says it is common to have guests come up with unusual special requests at the very last minute that can put a decided hint of challenge into the proceedings. Then, there are outdoor weddings that have to come inside because of rain; once she even had to deal with a snowstorm in May.

As the day of the event grows closer, Allan begins to get together a number of lists and schedules to keep track of all the different elements that go into the creation and execution of a banquet menu. The lists of special and unusual items need to be researched, to be sure that the kiln-dried figs and fresh enoki mushrooms will be available. Deliveries of other items that are readily available through ordinary purveyors must be scheduled so that goods will arrive as they are needed, without overburdening the available storage space too badly. Stocks, basic preparations for hors d'oeuvres, and the wedding cake are started in advance.

Allan also needs to schedule staff—perhaps even hire some additional staff for a day or two—according to the number of guests to be served at the reception and the style of service. It is important to have a prioritized list of responsibilities prepared and a clear idea of where the progress of the event must be on any given day.

On the day of the event, Denise is the mistress of ceremonies in far more than name. If there is a burned-out light or a missing coatrack, chances are good that her name is the one that will be called out. It is essential that the preliminary work be completed in advance of the anticipated arrival of the first guest. This includes arranging and setting tables, assembling plenty of clean ashtrays, matches, and napkins, polishing plenty of glassware and flatware, checking the flowers in the ladies' room and the soap container in the men's room, and placing the guest registry and a pen by the door to the banquet hall. Denise's checklist is long, but going through it carefully an hour before things get started saves her from cringing from across the room as a guest struggles out of a coat only to realize there's no place to put it.

Any caterer or banquet chef could regale you for hours with stories of near misses and worse. They may be funny after time has passed, but when a hysterical bride is staring you in the eye, they lose a great deal of their comedic potential. Not to mention that they do little to promote your image as a great caterer for a wonderful celebration.

Because most celebrations center on food, it is the duty of the kitchen, and hence the banquet chef, to set the pace of the event. The style and type of hors d'oeuvres service can be altered, even during the course of the reception, to allow more time or to speed the process along. If the bridal party is taking longer at the church than anticipated, Allan will adjust the service of hors d'oeuvres so that they will not be completely gone by the time the bridal party finally arrives, yet he must serve enough food so that the guests are not starved.

Buffet-style service should be arranged carefully so that the guests can walk easily around the buffet and back to their tables. There must be easy access to all foods, without having to reach over other dishes; this and a number of other considerations need to be kept in mind.

If the meal is to be served sit-down, Denise arranges for a suitable number of waiters so that service is prompt. The manager and the chef want to be sure that everyone gets served as quickly as possible; otherwise guests at some tables may be done eating while other guests still have not received their meals.

One of the final moments of concern for the banquet chef is the service of the wedding cake. It is important that there be enough time for proper ceremony, pictures, and all the rest, but at the same time, the kitchen or wait staff must be able to serve the cake as quickly as possible to the guests.

Private Catering

This is another to way to get into business with a limited amount of capital and low overhead expenses. Many people work out of their homes, providing food for other people's dinner parties, cocktail parties, receptions, baptisms, showers, and the myriad other events that call for a celebration with food.

One word of caution, however. There are probably health regulations that must be observed. If you are transporting prepared food, you will need a way to ensure that it is kept within the correct temperature range. You may also have to undergo an inspection of your kitchen to ensure that it is safe, sanitary, and up to code.

This can be an extremely exciting business; and, again, like bed-and-breakfasts, it is one that you can tailor to suit your own schedule. If you know that you want to take a vacation with your family in mid-March, you simply don't take on any parties at that time.

There are many different styles for caterers. Some people handle only small affairs that are catered directly in people's homes. They may make a ceiling of no more than fifty guests, for example. Limiting the number of guests allows caterers to hire the minimum number of employees they need to wait tables, prepare food, and mix drinks.

Other caterers like to handle larger affairs ranging from one hundred and up to one thousand or more. These large events take a great deal of strategy and planning, and usually there are fewer events of this size throughout the year. It becomes increasingly important to have a readily available source of temporary staff. If you are located in an area with a college, then you are probably in luck.

Where you live will have a direct influence on how busy you are and the kind of parties you will be able to find. Catering is also seasonal. Entertaining does happen in waves. The summer months are usually very busy, as are the months around the winter holidays. But there may be other busy times of the year in some areas. Try to find out as much as you can before placing an ad in the local newspaper.

If you have a booking for a large outdoor wedding reception at your client's home, you will need to visit the site to determine what kind of equipment you will need and whether you can devise a menu that will allow you to pull the event off without transporting portable refrigerators and stoves to the site.

You will undoubtedly need to rent chairs, tables, linen, china, and all the other necessary accoutrements for the event. If it is to be held outside, you need to determine if there should be tents. You will also need to look the site over carefully to determine if there will be sufficient parking for your staff and for the guests. You may need to bring in portable toilets as well. The amount of detail work required to come up with a complete list of rental items and menu is staggering, unless you are extremely organized.

You also need to be able to visualize the entire affair from beginning to end, mentally walking through all the phases of the reception. By doing that, you may find that you forgot to order trays or ice tubs for the drinks; beverage napkins; enough forks to get through a salad course, the entrée, and the dessert. If you are planning to give champagne to four hundred people and don't have champagne glasses, the chances of finding someone able to bail you out at the last moment are slim. But, if you have rehearsed how the party will run, you will have raised a champagne glass to give a toast, compared that action against one of your many lists, and realized the problem in time to avert disaster.

Another type of catering is geared directly to offices. You can offer a special service to offices. The way it works is this. You establish a contact in an office building and distribute a menu. The orders are placed by a specified time, and you prepare and deliver the food at a specified time as well. Your menu can be as diverse or a simple as you feel you can handle. Remember to give careful thought to how you will package and deliver the food before you branch out to too many offices, however. Cold food that should be hot and leaky brown paper bags do little to enhance your image. In addition to lunches, some caterers provide foods for coffee breaks in the morning and the afternoon.

Off-Premise Catering

Catering is a good way to stay involved in the food industry while keeping hours flexible and working from home. This can be an ideal solution for someone with small children or for someone who wants to combine part-time work with food with another primary career. Running a catering service from your own kitchen is not always the easiest thing to do, but it can be intensely stimulating, challenging, and rewarding.

Chris Sergeant, a young woman interested in becoming more involved in the food service industry, has built up a reliable list of clients who call on her to provide a whole host of services. One day she will prepare an elegant luncheon, deliver it to a client along with a huge bouquet of flowers, and come back several hours later to pick up the remains. The next day, she might be piling peanut butter and jelly sandwiches shaped like stars and hearts on platters for a child's birthday party, complete with a big cake decorated to look like the family dog. And the next week may find her preparing omelets for a family gathering to celebrate a fiftieth wedding anniversary.

When asked to explain how she got started and what type of advertising she uses, Chris says that she relies strictly upon word of mouth. She worked for a local catering shop and met a few people. They hired her for a small summer barbecue, and a couple who attended that party called her later to help with their son's surprise graduation party. There are times when nothing much is happening, but as she nears the busy season of late spring and summer, Chris can count on at least one big event every two weeks and several smaller ones sandwiched in between.

Setting fees is one of the biggest challenges for many people starting their own businesses. You don't want to scare away potential customers by charging too much, but, then again, you do have to be professional enough to charge what you are worth. The exact dollar amount will vary from one region to another, and there are a great many ways to arrive at the selling price for a catered event. Chris uses her own special technique. She calculates as closely as possible what it would cost to go to a restaurant or take-out shop for the meal. Then, she adds a fee for any rental items of paper goods (napkins, plates, glasses, or flatware) as well as additional staff. Finally, she calculates a percentage that she will find an acceptable bottom line for her earnings. All these figures are totaled, and a final bill is presented. Along the way, Chris has learned that you must remember to charge for the time spent developing menus, shopping, and arranging for the delivery of rented chairs or linens, flowers, and other amenities. Chris gained most of her knowledge through the school of hard knocks. Today, she recommends taking a course at a local vo-tech school to learn basic principles of business, accounting, and billing. Running your own business can be a confusing snarl, and it may even make sense to hire an accountant to help with a variety of problems.

Specialty Goods

Randi Foreman has recently returned to the workforce after a number of years spent raising her daughter. Now, she works a variety of positions, but her favorite work is baking homemade items to sell at a stand at a local farmer's market. She got a start by picking the wealth of fresh berries growing in her backyard and making them into her locally famous muffins. As the berries went out of season, she expanded her repertoire. She introduced some special whole wheat and carrot muffins, wonderfully chewy chocolate chip cookies, and melt-in-your mouth brownies. Once the market was over for the year, she took her wares around and found a few local restaurants interested in carrying her special, home-baked goodies.

Another intriguing approach has been taken by a couple in Missouri. When their catering business slowed down during the winter and early spring, they decided to offer a very special service, which they called Frozen Assets. They prepare two different soups in large batches and freeze them in containers that serve one, two, or more. They also bake quick breads and muffins and other easy-to-freeze and microwave items. They provide a new menu to their clients every two weeks and fill their orders.

Baked goods, special salads, salad dressings, and other special items featured in take-out shops and restaurants may well be prepared by individuals who supply one or more outlets. Some restaurant owners use this same technique to capitalize on their own reputations at the same time that they help themselves make it through a slow spell in the business. Craig and Abby Chasky of the Underhill Inn began by bottling and selling their raspberry vinaigrette. They have since expanded their line and offer several different sauces, marinades, and dressings. Their products are offered in such retail stores as Macy's and Dean & DeLuca. Craig is also investigating the possibility of packaging and selling his special handmade ice creams.

Vendors

Vendors may be independent operators or franchise holders, or they may be employed by a large company with multimillion-dollar contracts. They specialize in all sorts of events, such as athletic competitions, fairs, and conventions, as well as receptions, banquets, and street food. We've all seen those trucks that are parked by the side of the road or the carts that line the streets of most cities. The foods they offer range from hot dogs with "the works" to more exotic items, such as kebabs, croissants, even Creole dishes. In fact, there is practically no limit to the kinds of foods that street vendors are able to produce and sell from their trucks or carts.

The earning potential for this kind of business is higher than you might imagine. Some people work only part of the year and use their earnings to spend the remaining months of the year on vacation or living at their second homes. Don't write off this legitimate business opportunity. Some people eventually run a fleet of lunch wagons, making enough money to give the owner of an upscale restaurant reason to stop and think about what he or she ever thought was wrong with lunch wagons. In a society that does more things on the run than it ever did before, a service that allows people to stop for food on the way to the gym, or that comes directly to the work site, is a great boon.

Each town and city has different regulations governing how many lunch trucks there can be, where they can be located, and other considerations. Be sure to find out all the small details before you invest in the wagon. And do plenty of research on traffic patterns, what people normally do on the way to work and during their lunch hours, before you pick out your territory.

CHAPTER FIVE

Owning Your Own Place

Many people hold a special dream. They want to run their own place some day. They want to be in charge and do it the "right way," which is to say, their own way. With every job they have working for someone else, they tuck away ideas about what they would do, or wouldn't do, if they only had their own place.

In this chapter, we will look at some of the types of operations you might own or manage. This work takes a very special kind of personality. You need more self-motivation, stamina, endurance, and resourcefulness than you might ever imagine. You may prepare yourself for this challenging but rewarding venture by managing a restaurant for someone else. Or you may simply undertake the challenge with no previous experience.

Owning a restaurant means that you are responsible for every detail, from the china on the tables to the uniforms on the wait staff, from the fish delivery to the advertising copy. You may be pulled in some totally unexpected directions. As a member of the business community, you will look for ways to participate in the community—a wise move for a savvy businessperson, which is what you must be now. In order to meet the challenges and demands of restaurant ownership, you need a good support network, plenty of problem-solving skills, good public relations skills, and the ability to train and inspire your staff. It's a tall order, one that can only be met by taking full advantage of everything you've learned in all your other jobs and by constantly keeping your focus on providing the kind of service you want to be known for.

Owning Your Own Restaurant

This is the dream of a lifetime for many people. And those who have managed to achieve this dream will be the first to say that their dreams could not possibly approach the reality of dealing with the day-to-day drama of restaurant operation.

Whether you are the proud owner of a small bistro or a large steak house, you will find that, even more than as an employee, you are at the mercy of the paying public. No one can accurately predict what will work and what will not. There is simply no guarantee that the restaurant will be a success. The rate of failure for restaurants is incredibly high.

Before going into business for yourself, you should try to give yourself every possible advantage. Do a market analysis to find out if there are potential customers. Talk to other business owners in the area and try to get a feel for when business might be good, and when it might slow down. Consider your location carefully. Is it easily accessible, or will your guests get lost on the way to your door? Can they park once they get there? What is the neighborhood like?

Have someone you trust, and who really knows about construction, plumbing, and electricity, look over the building you are about to buy. Most likely, you will need to hire someone to do this, so don't be shy about asking other people who have restaurants if they can make recommendations. Hire a professional to watch over the construction of a new building, if you are starting from scratch. There are so many potential problems that it is impossible to begin to list them all. But be aware that things can go wrong, and they do go wrong. Boilers can stop working on the coldest night of the year, and, in fact, that is when they stop. Air conditioners can blow out on a hot summer night during a wedding reception, and the well can run dry during your busiest Sunday brunch ever. You, and your partners, if any, should plan to spend more money on getting the business ready to open than you ever imagined you would.

Learn about the permits, licenses, and inspections you will need to have done. Your business will affect the surrounding area, and you may have something in mind for your restaurant that is not allowed, according to the current zoning ordinance. Before you build a patio and order umbrellas, find out if outside seating is allowed.

Getting all of this information together will take time and money. Look at it as an investment in your future and the future of your business. And, remember, even with as much research as you can manage to do, turning every possible stone and reading every possible code, there will be unpredictable events. You could be open for a month only to lose your power for a week due to an untimely blizzard.

The owner of a restaurant is the person who works the hardest weeks, the longest days. He or she has to deal with wait staff, bartenders, purveyors, kitchen staff, and dishwashers. He or she is the one who has to root around in the basement at three in the morning to find enough champagne glasses for tomorrow's wedding reception. But, the owner is also the one who garners the greatest benefit and the most satisfaction from the work.

Inns and Bed-and-Breakfasts

Inns and bed-and-breakfast establishments offer a combination of lodging and meals to guests. Some inns are ultraelegant and offer a variety of services. Others provide nothing more elaborate that a comfortable bed with clean sheets, a shared bath, and a country-style breakfast. There can be a large staff, or it may be a mom-and-pop operation.

For many people, especially couples, this is an ideal entrée to the field. You need a large home with at least one extra bedroom and a place to serve breakfast to your guests. With those minimal requirements met, you can think about opening a B & B.

There are likely to be numerous applications to file with various local and state agencies and ordinances to find out about. You may need special licenses, and you may have to apply for a zoning variance. Be sure to do your homework thoroughly first.

There are several distinct advantages to running a bed-and-breakfast. You can determine when you will be open. If there is a time of year when you don't wish to work, you simply don't take any reservations. Breakfast is traditionally the only meal served, so once that meal has been taken care of, the rest of the operation would revolve around housekeeping chores—cleaning rooms and baths, changing linens—and bookkeeping chores.

Occasionally a B & B will decide to offer limited dining service. Guests staying at the bed-and-breakfast and, in some cases, guests who come simply for dinner will make a reservation. Quite often there is a set menu and fixed seating. In this way, the chef can plan very accurately how much food to prepare, and the workload can be scheduled to make the best use of everyone's time.

The disadvantage is that you will have someone in your home. This is a situation that is easier for some people to deal with than others. If you are a very private person, you may want to consider carefully how you would feel about having strangers walking through the rooms of your house, perusing your bookshelves, and admiring family photographs.

Other Special Businesses

Obviously there are more types of businesses than were mentioned here. Some may have been touched on briefly elsewhere in this book. Others may still be stashed away in the fertile imagination of a reader like you. The chances are there, if you have the courage, the luck, and the determination to make them real.

CHAPTER SIX

The Chef in Private Practice

*I*t is easy to forget that there are several thousand people working in the food service industry who do not report to a restaurant or hotel kitchen every day. The situations we will look at in this chapter are some of the most intriguing positions open to a talented chef. Many of them involve working for individuals, families, or private corporations. The chef who works in private placement or consultation may operate on a one-to-one basis, similar to a personal fitness trainer. In fact, chefs who can provide a very special service, tailored to meet the needs of an individual, are increasingly in demand.

Finding a job in the private sector can take more effort than finding other jobs. You may have to work through an agency, or you may have to rely on word of mouth. These jobs are not usually advertised in the help-wanted section of the newspaper. And it does take a certain temperament in order to make a go of it. You may find, after a time, that you feel stifled or even trapped working for the same two, three, or four people day in and day out.

However, you may find that this is the perfect chance to let your creativity soar. The chance to create a new menu daily with only the market as your limit, or a few pet peeves or allergies to set the boundaries, might be the kind of environment that makes you happiest.

There is no typical private-placement job. You may be simply the cook, with relatively little interaction with the family that you feed, or you may become an invaluable part of the household, a special "family member." It can be quite a challenge to have to pick up and go to a foreign country when the family decides to go on vacation, but if you find the idea appealing, look into it some more, and give it a try.

In-Home Personal Chef

The rich and famous among us often have household staffs that include one or more chefs. The First Family has a private chef; the mayor of New York City has a private chef as well. There are plenty of other individuals and families who employ a private chef, and they are not all high-ranking political officials or CEOs of *Fortune* 500 companies. Some of these families, couples, or individuals are simply extremely busy with their own careers. They find that having someone to prepare their meals, do the shopping, and take care of the kitchen for them is as economically reasonable as hiring a service to clean their homes and sending their laundry out. Whenever time is valuable, a private chef becomes a reasonable alternative to dining out constantly.

As you might imagine, the range of responsibilities for a private chef will vary greatly from one situation to another, as will the compensation. John Falls, a horticulturist by trade with a passion for both flowers and food, has managed to secure beautiful housing in a furnished cottage in exchange for cooking a few meals each week and keeping the flower beds manicured. This arrangement leaves him plenty of time to run his own thriving landscaping company, while satisfying his desire to cook fine food (not to mention living on a lovely estate without having to pay rent or utilities).

Another private chef, Thomas Schroeder, has a different arrangement. After graduating from the Culinary Institute of America, he followed the same career path as many of his classmates. However, after he and his wife had their second child, it seemed like a good time to make a change. He looked for a very special situation, working for a family, that required him to cook primarily on weekends at the family's upstate residence and once or twice a week in their New York City town house. They entertain lavishly, and he is in charge of all aspects, along with the family's majordomo (steward). In return for all of this highly skilled work, he receives housing for himself and his family, medical and dental insurance, a car to conduct business for the family, and a salary as well.

Working for a family is not always perfect, however, and a great deal of adjustment is necessary on the part of the chef. Your schedule may be regular as clockwork, or you may never know from week to week, or even day to day or meal to meal, what the future might hold. Let's examine a few different scenarios.

You may find yourself on call; let's imagine that the couple you work for went out to a party and came home very late. They may wake you so that you can prepare them omelets. Or you may have enough food in the house to make lunch for the couple, their children, and the two guests who were there for breakfast—only to find out that several other friends dropped by in the course of a morning horse ride. You must remain incredibly flexible, as well as being truly ingenious when it comes to repeating the miracle of the loaves and fishes.

Your function may include other responsibilities. The duty of doing all the shopping for the household may fall to you as well. In addition to overseeing the operation of the kitchen, you may also function as the majordomo. This means that you might be the one who makes out schedules and manages the operation of the entire household staff.

Or you may be looked to as the sommelier. This would mean you would be required to match wines to the foods selected for a particular menu. You might also be looked to for advice or guidance in selecting and purchasing wines for the cellar.

Menu planning may be strictly your domain, or you may work in conjunction with the family. It will always be necessary to suit the menu to the personal likes and dislikes of the family members, as well as their guests. Many people will require or prefer a special diet, low in sodium and cholesterol, for example, or vegetarian. It becomes increasingly important to know how to meet the expectations of your employer without repeating a cycle of meals in an endless rotation.

Entertaining may well take up a large portion of your time. This may mean hiring additional staff, coordinating florists, musicians, and a host of other people hired for a particular occasion. The ability to stay organized in the face of overwhelming chaos may be one of the most valuable tools you can bring to the job.

Working for a family is not for everyone. The benefits may be great. There is a chance that you will travel to beautiful, exotic places. You may find that you are actually working for the family for what amounts to no more than a third to a fourth of the year. But, unlike a restaurant, where you can get up and go at the end of the day, you will most likely live directly in the house, or near enough so that you can be available almost on a moment's notice. You may occasionally feel that you have become more of a caretaker than a chef, responsible for packing school lunches, picking up dry cleaning, and doing other domestic chores that simply are not part of the job description for someone working in a restaurant or hotel.

Look carefully at what the trade-offs will be before making a decision. This type of work is incredibly fulfilling and rewarding under the right circumstances, and with the right personalities involved. By all means, however, take the time to ask a lot of questions and let the family find out about you first.

Chef on a Yacht

This sounds like one of the most alluring jobs that you could ever find. Imagine yourself drifting along on the beautiful Caribbean Sea, dropping anchor off an exotic island, and preparing exotic foods with mangoes and papayas.

Just to be fair, though, consider this picture, too. You are at sea for long stretches, and keeping food fresh in a tiny galley with limited refrigeration and storage is going to be a serious concern. The people on board, whether they own the boat or have simply rented it, will consider meals one of their favorite forms of entertainment. You can't go very far or do very much on a boat, and neither can they. The sea can get choppy, and the food is as likely to take a spill on the floor as the charts are.

You should also realize that you can't take a day off. While you are sailing around on the ocean, you will be on call, all day, every day. This can get a little exasperating, especially after a late night "kitchen raid" followed by an early breakfast, a midmorning snack, and then lunch. Just as you get started on full-scale dinner preparations, wondering all the time if sleep deprivation inflicts permanent, irreversible damage, someone will come down to the galley to ask if you could make a little something to tide them over until the hors d'oeuvres you have planned for happy hour.

Now that you've considered some of the downsides, think again about the sea breezes, the exotic ports of call, and the thrill of living on a boat. Most chefs who work on charter boats can decide which cruises they will take and how long they will be at sea. You can have at least a little control over how much of your life is spent as a "galley slave." And, if you work on very large boats, you will not be alone in the galley.

Some people own their own boats and act as both crew and chef. This is especially true of young couples in the Caribbean and other romantic waterways. They may offer a whole range of services, from honeymoon cruises to special cruises for small families who just want to unwind on the open water. Because they own the boat, they can decide where to drop anchor and for how long between cruises, when they want to work, and when they want to enjoy the good life on a boat all by themselves.

Not every chef on a boat is working in the balmy environment of the Caribbean. There are plenty of other boats and plenty of other opportunities. Andre Ostermeir, a young man who had just graduated from cooking school, elected to take a job working on a boat that was an offshore site for oil drilling in the Arctic Ocean. His schedule on the boat was heavy—three meals a day for two separate shifts for three weeks at a stretch with no days off. Then, he would come ashore for three weeks, ticket in hand, able to travel wherever he wanted to spend his time off.

So if it still sounds worth the trouble, look into it. There is almost always an opportunity, because the romance of the sea is not always enough for everyone when they face the reality. For others, though, it is a great way to find adventure while earning a living.

Executive Dining Chef

The opportunity to work as the chef for an executive dining room may perfectly suit to some people. The hours are generally regular and seldom will extend past the lunch hour. The number of people you will be cooking for is often quite small.

Many of the same requirements demanded of a private chef are also necessary to be successful when working as the chef for an executive dining room. Here, too, you will need to be able to accommodate the needs and desires of a select group of readily identifiable personalities. The style of the company may be reflected in the kinds of foods preferred in the lunchroom. A young, contemporary business may favor trendy foods. A conservative, well-established corporation may cling to the traditions of a men's club—red meat, not too many vegetables, and cold martinis. Or the company may prefer a simple approach to its meals.

It is essential to be able to tailor the menu to the group of people you will be serving. And it is equally important to keep in mind that time is a critical commodity in almost every aspect of business. The meals must be served punctually. In cases where business is conducted at the meal, there must also be a minimum of disruption from wait staff. More than likely it will be preferable to select foods that won't make a mess out of business papers and silk ties. Look at it as a challenge!

There are fewer opportunities to impress a large audience than you might have working for a restaurant or a hotel, but there are a great many more holidays and weekends open to spend with your family or friends. For some people, this type of position represents a chance to continue their educations or to branch out slowly into business for themselves.

Another possibility is that you might find yourself in an exotic clime, working at corporate headquarters. There are pluses and minuses to this type of work, as Thomas Lyons might be the first to tell you. He works for a company that has a compound in a major city in Yemen, where executives from branch offices come for meetings and rest and relaxation. His job is to make them feel pampered and also to help alleviate a little bit of homesickness by offering meals that will remind everyone of their homes back in the States. It can be difficult, and the logistics of ordering supplies and making sure that there are enough items to last between the deliveries is a constant worry, but, like the chef marooned on a boat in the Arctic Ocean for three weeks, he gets substantial chunks of time off, along with an airline ticket to whatever area sounds interesting. Since he has been with this company, he has visited Cairo, some of the Greek Islands, and London.

Shopping and Menu Planning Service

Families in which both partners are involved in their careers often want the satisfaction of preparing meals, but they simply do not have the time that it takes to sit down and plan out a week's meals and then do the necessary shopping. The types of services you might offer clients can be quite diverse. You might include shopping, menu planning, preparatory work, or any combination of the three. In this case, clients should tell you clearly their preferences, needs, and any special concerns. After an initial review of the foods they currently eat that fit in with the diet program outlined by a doctor or a trained nutritionist, you might then go into their kitchens to get a feel for what kinds of foods they have on hand. Some people offering this kind of service actually "clean house," removing all the "bad" foods and outfitting the kitchen with a completely new "good" pantry, refrigerator, and freezer.

After this initial work is completed, the service may develop a weekly menu, which then generates a shopping list. The food is purchased, delivered, and unpacked.

This type of service is gaining in popularity, especially in larger metropolitan areas. The number of clients that your service can handle will depend on how well you can organize your work and dovetail shopping and delivery schedules.

You need to have the necessary creativity to devise weekly menus for the same client week in and week out, month in and month out, without repeating the same dishes over and over. Nothing is less appealing than a steady diet of plain chicken breast, rice, steamed broccoli, and poached pears.

You may find that you need to learn more about special ingredients or ethnic cuisines. It may help to find out what restaurants your clients enjoy, what their favorite "comfort" foods are, and anything else that can help you in the all-important work of coming up with those meal plans.

Menu Planning and Meal Preparation Service

Many of the same requirements just noted apply here as well, with the important addition that the food is already prepared, fully or partially, when it is delivered to the house. This means that the client will simply reheat the entrée—usually in a microwave—toss the prepared salad greens with the prepared salad dressing, and put dinner on the platter or plates.

It is important to take time at first to assess how much time it will take you to meet each client's needs. Making enough stock or soup to deliver to your clients will take about the same amount of time whether you are making a batch for ten or a batch for thirty. But when you have to debone, skin, trim, and pound chicken breasts, each one takes the same amount of time, multiplied by the number of times you have to do it.

This service may also require that you make deliveries twice or even three times throughout the week, in order to be sure that the food is at the peak of freshness, flavor, and quality. The added travel time, cost of gasoline, and wear and tear on your vehicle need to be accounted for when you work out your own schedule and fees.

The Total Service

In some areas of the country, there is demand for fitness and nutrition consultants who will visit clients' homes to see that they exercise appropriately and eat the right foods at the right time. This service offers the best of all health worlds.

A personal exercise trainer ensures that the type and amount of exercise is geared especially to the abilities and needs of the individual. And since health is a question of balance, it is important that this toned, strengthened body is fed the right nutrients, in the right portions, and at the right time.

CHAPTER SEVEN

Teaching Cooking

One of the places to begin a cooking career is the classroom, giving instruction in the fundamentals as well as the more advanced techniques used in cooking and baking. In this chapter, we will take a look at some of the ways that a love of teaching and a love of cooking can be combined into a rewarding career.

Private Cooking Lessons

Melissa Flood, a former dining room manager and private chef, has worked for many years giving private cooking lessons designed to suit the needs of a single individual. When she was working as the chef of a small winery in upstate New York, many of the regular visitors to the dining room clamored for instruction in preparing some of Melissa's famous soups, grilled entrées, and inspired salads. Instead of teaching her tricks to a large group, she prefers to tailor the material to the needs, ability, and taste of a single person.

Frequently, these lessons are a gift from a spouse or a close friend. Melissa remembers one situation in particular, where a young couple, about to start life together after they got married, made a vow to each other to stay as healthy and fit as possible. One of the ways they felt they could reach this goal was to learn to cook healthy, nutritious foods. Neither one was willing to live on brown rice and sprouts and beans, so they looked for inspiration in some of their favorite restaurants. Melissa's menu, selected from the freshest local ingredients she could find, and tied as closely to the seasons as possible, seemed like a logical approach. After hearing the bride admire the food at the winery on many occasions, her mother decided to give her daughter a series of lessons with Melissa as a wedding gift.

"We began with some real basics, like how to pick out a good knife, how to choose the right knife for the right job, and how to keep it safe and sharp. Then, on another day, we went to the market, and I showed her exactly what I look for in a variety of foods when I am buying them. I explained how I let the food create the menu, rather than coming into the store with a list based on a recipe I pulled out of some book and then coming home with nothing because the items I wanted weren't in the store.

"Then, we started cooking. I firmly believe that even a home cook should prepare plenty of stock—chicken stock, fish stock, and vegetable stock—and keep it on hand in the freezer. This is a very easy task, and I talked a lot about how to make it into a once-a-month operation. While the stocks were simmering away, I suggested that we spend some time looking through cookbooks, magazines, and newspapers to come up with ideas and inspirations for future menus. There is a lot of thinking that goes on in a well-run kitchen, and I talked about that quite a bit. Like how you could prepare bread doughs for pizzas while long-cooking items simmer on the stove or braise in the oven.

"Next, we tackled some special foods that need care and meticulous attention: fresh produce, some grains, and beans. Finally we moved on to a few quick sautéed and grilled dishes that featured fish and lean poultry. All told, the series of classes took about two months, with eight lessons. It was a wonderful learning experience. We always worked in her kitchen, with her equipment, and paid attention to her personal likes and dislikes. Cooking needs to be a fun project, one that you can approach with a sense of joy. Knowing the situation of a particular student and how they like to eat and entertain makes it possible for me to custom fit the things I teach."

In a society where fewer and fewer of us are learning to cook by standing next to our parents as they prepare the evening meal, the tradition of home cooking gets lost quickly. Some people can learn to cook from magazine articles and illustrated books. But, there is something tactile and immediate about cooking that needs a few words of wisdom gained from years spent whipping up a perfect rice pilaf or tossing the ultimate Caesar salad. That just doesn't come through, except in person.

If you are one of those people who seems to always be on the phone giving a little hint about this recipe or a suggestion or two about how to use that bumper crop of basil to best advantage, you might be just the right kind of person to give personal cooking lessons. It can be a little awkward at first, charging someone for instruction in cooking. The more you are used to answering a zillion questions from friends and family about how to cook this or bake that, the harder it will be to break the mold. Take a professional approach, and try not to get sidetracked, and eventually you will find your own personal teaching style.

The only real qualifications for teaching private cooking lessons are that you be a good cook yourself, and organized enough to explain the process logically and in enough detail so that someone else can follow your directions and produce a good end result. Some of the classes that are usually very popular are those that focus on a special type of cooking. For example, if yeast breads are your specialty, you might offer a few classes on basic breads, and then follow them up with more difficult items. Or you might offer a person faced with organizing a special dinner party one or more sessions on how to plan a menu and make the right lists, how to stagger the work so that it gets done on time without leaving the host feeling dead tired on the night of the big event; you might even offer practice runs in preparing a special chicken dish or an elaborate chocolate dessert.

This type of work is ideal for someone who is happiest when working flexible hours. You can tailor a class to suit both your needs and those of a special client. You can even be flexible about where the class is taught. It might be most reasonable to teach the class in your student's home. Or it might vary from class to class, situation to situation. While it is certainly possible to make a living at this type of work, most people find that they can handle a few students, teach about three to four classes a week, and keep enough energy and interest in their work to keep from getting burned out.

Advertising for this type of instruction can range from the extremely informal, word-of-mouth variety to a more professional approach that includes flyers or print ads in local papers and magazines.

Group Lessons

Another woman, Dale Kahn of Clinton Comers, New York, offers special classes in cake decorating. She has a fairly well-established list of courses, including such specialties as marzipan flowers and royal icing work. These classes grew out of the publicity that she received for her fabulously decorated wedding cakes. After a local paper featured her confectionery creations, she was deluged by requests to learn the way that she formed the beautiful flowers, filigree, and latticework that decorated her masterpieces. Her classes are limited to suit the work space that she has available, and the students spend five to seven days watching demonstrations and practicing the craft. Each community may have some special regulations governing how an individual can be approved for an in-home school permit, if one is necessary. Contact the town hall or chamber of commerce to learn the proper procedure. This is an important step. Imagine your embarrassment if your classes really catch on and you are featured in a newspaper, only to have the health authorities arrive at your door the next day to shut you down.

Many well-known cookbook authors began their careers by teaching cooking from their homes. Ken Hom, a noted author of several award-winning cookbooks, and Betty Rosbottom, cookbook author and founder of La Belle Pomme cooking school, are two such individuals. They took a genuine love for cooking and the ability to explain and instruct, and they began with a few classes. As they became more popular, they added more courses, upgraded their kitchens, and bought professional-caliber equipment. Eventually, they created the ultimate long-distance teaching tool—a cookbook.

Perhaps one of the most influential of all teachers who conducted cooking classes in her home was Simone Beck, known by many as "Simca." Her training as a cook included time spent under the tutelage of chef and author, Henri-Paul Pellaprat. Twenty years later, she formed a partnership with another famous author and teacher, Julia Child, in the late 1950s. Together, they opened L'École des Trois Gourmandes in Paris. Until very shortly before her death in 1992, she continued to teach cooking in her home in the south of France. It was her belief that "you must never stop learning, because every day I discover something new—even in my old age."

A bona fide cooking school requires a curriculum, no matter how limited the course offerings. You will need to prepare an outline of the course in advance so that the appropriate promotion and advertising can be prepared. Flyers, brochures, and even radio ads might be appropriate. Students need to know what type of classes they can choose from, so a brief description should be prepared. They also need to know in advance what the fees will be, what tools they should bring from their homes, if any, and any other special items that might be required. A class in cake decorating, for example, might require the student to bring two or three prebaked cake layers. The size of the group may dictate some modifications or changes in your current kitchen, making it more convenient for several people to work on foods at once or simply increasing storage space to handle the additional foods that will be required.

Unlike a private lesson where the cost can be determined by the cost of foods being cooked or the amount of time spent, there is usually a well-defined cost to the student for a group course. You may want to specify that students bring their own knives and aprons, or you may provide all foods and tools that will be used in the course. Remember as you prepare the prices that you will be using more electricity, cooking gas, and water. You should factor those overhead costs into the cost of the course. After all, the idea is to make money, not just to provide a service!

There is a degree of flexibility built into this work, and you can tailor the hours to work around the needs of your other interests, a second (or primary) career, or a growing family. However, it is important that, once the class schedule is prepared and printed, you be able to fulfill the promise implicit in such a written proposal.

Demonstrations and Classes in Stores

Specialty shops that feature cookware and gourmet items will often provide cooking demonstrations to attract customers. These demonstrations may be offered to the shop by manufacturers or wholesalers of a particular item as a means of promoting their product lines.

Not everyone appearing in front of a crowd in a white jacket and a tall hat is a working professional chef. It may be the garb that you are asked to don in your role as demonstration chef. You may be given a script, or you may be asked to develop a program based on the specific needs of whoever is paying your fee. If you are doing a demonstration to promote a special line of cookware, for instance, you will most likely have to cook several types of foods in order to show off the special capabilities of that line.

Not all of these demonstrations are done in shops. They may also be held at "home parties" where a group of potential customers will gather at the host's home for a cooking demonstration and then (it is to be hoped) will order the products you are promoting.

To find out about such job opportunities, contact stores in your area that cater to the gourmet, and see if they already offer cooking demonstrations. If they don't, you can write a proposal. Sue Caterson, who currently owns her own gourmet shop in a small town in Connecticut, got her start by doing a few sessions a month featuring Chinese cooking. Another resource is to do some background searching to find out how manufacturers of special food items or cookware handle promotion. If they do offer demonstrations in shops or at home-and-living expositions sponsored by communities, then you can write to ask for more information and to do a little promotion of your own.

Demonstrations and Classes for Community Groups

Many towns and cities throughout the country offer a variety of cooking classes as part of an adult education series provided through the high school, vocational school, junior college, or centers such as the YW/YMCA. These classes usually focus on certain specialties. Susan Hill, a young woman who earns her living as a waitress and aerobics instructor, also fulfills another of her dreams by teaching classes in vegetarian cuisine and basic bread making at the local YMCA in Poughkeepsie, New York. She isn't exactly making enough there to retire on, but it does fill a special niche in her life. In addition, she has made many contacts for her catering gigs. Some of these are done out of her home; for larger parties, she has made an arrangement to use the commercial equipment in the Y's kitchen.

Schools for Professional Chefs

A number of schools around the country offer associate's or bachelor's degrees that focus exclusively on the food service industry. One of the most famous is the Culinary Institute of America, located in Hyde Park, New York. This school was founded by Frances Roth in 1946. She worked in conjunction with the New Haven (Connecticut) Restaurant Association to begin a school that could train GIs returning from World War II to fill the many jobs in the restaurant industry that were going begging. Mrs. Roth came to the work with a reputation for her ability to succeed at difficult tasks. Her background included such credits as being the first woman to belong to the Connecticut Bar Association and serving as a prosecuting attorney for the state. She was joined by another dynamic and resourceful woman, Katharine Angell, who established a reference library and student-aid fund for needy students.

From its beginnings in a storefront in New Haven, the school has grown by leaps and bounds. It moved in 1973 to its current campus on the banks of the Hudson River. The school's faculty of around ninety-five chefs and related instructors offers students a collective bank of experience that totals nearly two thousand years.

Most instructors come to this type of work after spending several years working in the field. Usually, they have worked as an executive chef or pastry chef, dining room manager, or have completed a master's degree or better in a related field. The curriculum at the Culinary Institute of America covers several diverse areas, and the talented and able faculty can readily accommodate students' needs. Michael Weiss, wines instructor, has achieved recognition in his special field, the study and service of wines. Chef instructors like Jonathan Zearfoss have trained under such notable chefs as Marcel DeSaulniers at the Trellis.

Becoming an instructor has a special appeal. For an executive chef with a family, it is a chance to work fairly regular hours that leave time for raising children. On a professional level, the regular hours allow chefs time to perfect their own skills in a setting that brings chefs together in a single spot, fostering the give-and-take of information and experience that can create a rich and multileveled learning experience for faculty and students alike.

CHAPTER EIGHT

Research and Development

R esearch and development covers a broad spectrum within the food service industry and includes exciting job opportunities. Here are options for those who aren't interested in restaurant work but who want the satisfaction of a job related to their favorite hobbies—food, wine, and the enjoyment of both. Although the opportunities outlined in this chapter might seem on the outer fringes of the food service industry, these jobs are important to those in the mainstream of the industry and satisfying to those who hold them.

What are these jobs? Many different organizations make use of testing and development kitchens, from magazines to product manufacturers to companies that design software for chefs and cooks. The work done in these kitchens will vary depending on the organization. A nutrition newsletter will want to develop recipes that are nutritious and in full compliance with a set of nutritional guidelines. A company that produces microwaves will want to develop recipes that make the best use of the ovens that they produce.

Work schedules in the field of research and development are as diverse as the work itself. If you are flexible and prefer to work on a freelance basis, you can find great numbers of opportunities. Very often, companies, individuals, or groups need work on a project-by-project basis. This arrangement can be ideal for someone who is not interested in a full-time position.

Other research jobs are, of course, full-time positions, and if you love to do the detailed work and the writing they involve, research and development could be the field for you.

Working for a Magazine Test Kitchen

A number of magazines provide recipes to their readers, but not every one actually tests the recipes carefully. Those that do have a distinct advantage over those that don't because the sources for most recipes are not necessarily 100 percent accurate. The recipe might be the half-remembered main course of a dinner enjoyed at a little restaurant in Mexico, more than a decade ago. Or the chef who wrote it down might be thinking in terms of how the dish would be prepared in her professionally organized kitchen, not a home kitchen where stocks are not necessarily prepared daily. Or the recipe may have been sent in by a reader, along with a request to make it work better than it does right now.

First, the recipe is tested exactly as it is received. Let's say that a chef provides a recipe for pumpkin soup. The first trial run should lead you to ask a number of questions. Are the measurements accurate? Did you get a texture and taste that you and your tasters found appealing? If not, what needs adjusting? Do you have to use homemade stock? What might happen if you used bouillon cubes? Can you use frozen pumpkin? What are some additional ways to garnish the dish? What would you serve with it? And so on.

After answering as many question as possible, the recipe is tested again, and then again, until a recipe that produces consistent and tasty results emerges. Testers strike a balance between literal interpretation of the existing recipe and creative, intuitive reactions to the way that the finished dish tastes and looks. All in all, it is an interesting and challenging enterprise.

The next phase is writing the recipe clearly and precisely. The person reading the recipe in a magazine should be able to produce the exact same results that you got.

One of the most intriguing test kitchens is operated by a magazine called *Saveur*. The people who work in this test kitchen pull together a great many skills and talents in order to properly develop and edit a recipe for their magazine. Recipes published in

Saveur must meet the standards of the editorial staff. They must be true to the flavor, texture, and ingredients of the authentic regional dish. They must also adapt readily to the ingredients and equipment of cooks in the United States. Finding sources for exotic tools or ingredients and evaluating different brands or manufacturers is part of the job. Writing clear, concise notes for the editors is another. Add in the significant amount of research, checking, and double-checking done in person, on the Web, in a library, or at the local market, and you begin to see just how much challenge this career path offers.

Other publications will have different needs. Some may need to have recipes developed for a special theme, such as Valentine's Day or the Fourth of July. These special menus are often developed in conjunction with a feature article. Or a seasonal menu featuring a special ingredient or group of ingredients might be required. You may have to actually come up with an original recipe, scaled to serve four, or twelve, or maybe fifty, depending upon the event as well as the audience for the magazine. Sometimes, the magazine will select a theme, such as French cuisine, pasta, or Vietnamese cooking, for the entire issue. Or an article might be devoted to getting the most out of your food processor or explaining the mysteries of a pressure cooker. Canning and preserving foods and recipes for pickles and relishes might be next on the agenda. The schedule for most of this work is a little hectic, and you might find yourself roasting a goose for a Christmas issue sometime in July or searching for strawberries to feature in a springtime issue sometime in the late fall.

Recipe writing is far from an exact science, but the aim is to make certain the recipe is likely to produce the expected results when it is properly followed. Each audience will have different demands from a recipe, and that is part of what must be taken into account as you start the work of testing and, eventually, writing a recipe for publication in a magazine.

Each magazine has a typical audience, and that is a big clue as to how much expertise, if any, you can expect the reader to bring to the recipe itself. If you are working in the test kitchen maintained by a publication such as *Restaurant Business* magazine, you know that your readers are already in the food service industry. Certain terms and techniques will be familiar to them. Therefore, you don't have to spell out every single detail. Instead, you can use a more abbreviated jargon. However, if you are working in a test kitchen for *Good Housekeeping* or *Redbook*, then it is important to be very specific and to give exact measurements, temperatures, directions, and clear indications for determining when something is properly cooked.

Each publication will also have its own special style for recipe writing, and it is the tester's responsibility to make sure that the recipe is written down as carefully as possible, so that the editor can work with it, making any necessary stylistic changes.

People who get jobs in test kitchens usually have some experience with cooking. Many will have some schooling, either through a vocational or technical school or as a result of their work experiences. In addition to proven cooking skills, there may be some additional requirements. For instance, you may be asked to work with a food photographer as a stylist. Or you may need to be able to perform nutritional analyses of recipes. Investigate the journal you want to work with carefully to find out what special skills would make you a more appealing candidate. Communications skills, especially writing, are usually highly valued because you will need to explain in writing why a recipe, ingredient, product, or tool worked or didn't work. This need not be creative writing, and you may not have to produce columns. If you can, however, so much the better.

There is another intriguing area of work that involves research for magazines, newsletters, radio, and television programs. That is as a researcher or librarian. Michael Gold works as the researcher for the University of California at Berkeley *Wellness Letter*. As part of his work for this publication, he compiles and double-checks a staggering amount of research from a vast array of sources for the authors of the various articles. There are similar positions with most major publications and radio or television programs that have a food or health-related segment.

Other Test Kitchens

The companies and manufacturers that produce goods for the food service industry usually have state-of-the-art research and development kitchens, staffed with chefs and cooks. When General Foods introduces a new line of microwaveable entrées, or when Braun elects to market a new handheld mixing tool, a great deal of time, effort, and money is budgeted to develop the new product or product line from start to finish.

Imagine that your job is to help come up with about fifteen suggested entrée items that can be prepared, packaged, frozen, and then sold to the consumer. The consumer then takes these items home and prepares them in the microwave. What steps are involved? The initial phases might involve a lot of brainstorming and creative thinking. You would want to include foods that are popular, familiar, and delicious. Once you come up with an initial list of dishes, then you need to take time to find out how they will react during processing. If the green peppers in the Szechuan beef with peppers dish are turning gray and mushy after you freeze them, you need to come up with a solution. Will steaming them first help, or should you consider replacing the green peppers with broccoli? Then, you need to find out what the portion size ought to be. Much of this work will have to be done in conjunction with other experts. You may not know what the pricing strategy is supposed to be, but the marketing staff certainly will have a good idea. Then, you need to know what the bottom line is for food cost. Your company can't make a profit if the food that goes into the package costs nearly as much as the selling price.

Packaging will play a large role in this process, and you will need to work with the package designers. Even though you expect that most people will use their microwaves to prepare this food, some people won't have a microwave and will want to prepare the dish in a conventional oven. Will the packaging stand up to that type of heat? If not, can you the change the packaging or make suitable adjustments for nonmicrowave households?

A great deal of science is involved in this type of work. It is important to know what happens to foods when they are heated and cooled and how different additives and preservatives will affect the food. And, in today's world, it is a fairly sure bet that you will need to address nutritional concerns. You may have to do much of the nutritional analysis yourself, or you may need to work with a registered dietician. Some relatively new techniques for processing food, such as irradiation, *sousvide*, and cook-and-chill items that are shelf stable, have become important to the food-processing companies. These technical advances all have an effect on the way that foods are handled. They also have an effect on the way that consumers view the reliability and quality of the products your company prepares.

On top of some basic chemistry as it relates to food, you will also need to have a sufficient command of basic computer programs so that you can work effectively with other departments in your company and do the necessary research, prepare the essential reports, and communicate the vital data.

The research and development kitchens are very different from the production kitchens, where products are actually cooked in bulk quantities, treated, processed, packaged, and readied for shipping. There must be ongoing dialogue between these two kitchens, however, so that quality standards are met and a product that meets the expectations of both the company and the consumer is consistently, reliably, and safely prepared.

Companies that produce such foodstuffs as cereals, cornmeal, pancake mixes, canned fruits, gelatin desserts, and frozen vegetables often provide recipes on their packages as an aid to the consumer, as well as a gimmick to get them to select their brands over the competitors'. Very often, they will maintain testing kitchens where recipes are carefully tested and checked. These recipes must feature the product being promoted, of course. In many cases, the source for at least part of the recipes is a contest open to the public. This usually involves a great deal of preliminary screening, followed by the actual contest, where dishes are prepared for the judges' scrutiny. Once the prizes are awarded and the contest is over, the recipes belong to the company. One of the most famous of these contests, the Pillsbury Bakeoff, has been around for several decades.

As you can see, the skills required here vary widely. You need to be part scientist, part consumer advocate, part nutritionist, part computer whiz, and part chef. On top of that, you must be able to communicate the cooking directions for each item precisely, in the fewest possible words, creating the least possible occasion for confusing the consumer.

R & D for Special-Interest Groups

Many of the special recipes treasured by America's cooks come from the backs of boxes and the side panels of containers of all sorts of foods, from cornstarch to cocoa powder. Real live people are behind those recipes, developing them to appeal to consumers and writing them to fit into some pretty tight quarters. Large food producers such as General Foods and General Mills frequently have test kitchens devoted to coming up with new and interesting ways to use their products. And as many of their products find their way into a single recipe as possible.

But food manufacturers aren't the only ones who want to provide recipes as a service to their consumers. Various councils, such as the United States Rice Council or the Florida Citrus Growers Association, also have a vested interest in keeping their favorite commodities in the public eye, to promote sales and generate interest. One of the best ways to do this is to produce recipes, booklets, brochures, and educational material showcasing the best qualities of that food. In this case, a great deal of thought has to go into the recipes. Some recipes are aimed at the professional market or institutions that must feed several hundred people. The focus shifts when you are trying to tailor a recipe to meet the needs of a small family or, a growing concern today, singles or couples. Each audience will have a particular set of skills and equipment to draw on. The marketing and research arms of an organization may be there to tell you that the average consumer will lose interest if the recipe has more than seven ingredients or six steps. Or you may have to do some digging yourself to investigate how many pans the average person is willing to dirty to make a meal.

The company, council, or organization for which you work is likely to have some very specific goals in mind. In order to make yourself a good candidate for work in their kitchens, you will probably want to demonstrate cooking skills, research skills, some background in science and food chemistry, a knowledge of how to communicate effectively with a variety of audiences, and a good sense of what will work, with which type of audience. Much of this talent comes with experience, of course, but if this type of work interests you, learn to write a resume and cover letter that highlight any and all facets of your education and work experience that touch on these skills. Make yourself stand out in the crowd.

R & D for Manufacturers

When you come home with your brand new toaster oven, handheld blender, microwave, electric mixer, or food processor, you usually find a warranty, an operator's manual, and a recipe booklet tucked inside the box. Much of what you find in the operator's manual has been carefully checked out in the test kitchens, and all of the recipes and hints in the recipe booklet come from there.

For most people, these labor-saving tools are a pleasure to work with, but they can be a little intimidating if you have never actually owned a microwave or a five-quart mixer before. The people who put together the consumer instructions must be able to foresee what kinds of questions, problems, and accidents might develop while the machine is being set up or installed and then turned on for the first time. The appliance goes through numerous demonstrations with a variety of operators. They try to simulate everything they can think of that might happen under normal, and even not-so-normal, operation. They try to find out how the mixer will react with a heavy bread dough, or how evenly the microwave will thaw out a lump of frozen ground beef. They check to see if the handheld blender makes a smooth shake in a few minutes or a few seconds, and how long it takes the pressure cooker to come up to full pressure with a full recipe of soup inside.

Then, once answers to the nuts-and-bolts questions have been written down carefully so that the results can be presented to the average consumer, the next step is to develop recipes. After you've made rice pilaf, what else can you do with rice in a microwave? You might consult other cookbooks that specialize in microwave cookery to get some ideas. You might try taking a favorite recipe that you've always cooked the conventional way and adapting it to the microwave. And as you tinker with recipes from a variety of sources, making them as foolproof as possible, you will probably uncover a wealth of special techniques. These recipes and techniques must also be properly recorded in writing so they can be passed on to the ultimate audience.

Some appliance manufacturers like to provide demonstrations in stores that will carry their lines. Then, you might get to come out of the test kitchen and into the limelight, where you will show off the appliance and the recipes you or your coworkers have developed. In addition to putting on a show, you will need to be able to think quickly on your feet. The questions you will confront might make you wonder why you ever thought you had come up with every possible scenario as you practiced your presentation in front of the mirror.

For this job, you need to have an inventor's yen to tinker with equipment and get inside the "soul of the machine." The machinery, in this case, is intended to make the preparation of food easier and quicker, so that means you need to know how to cook. Maybe we aren't talking about world-class cuisine, but still it needs to be fresh, appealing, wholesome, and suitable for the families, couples, and budding gourmets who will buy the appliance. This is no small task, and it requires sound basic cooking skills, as well as some creative flair. And, of course, if demonstrations are in your future, showmanship, a good personality, and a nimble wit are all prerequisites as well.

Recipe Testing for Cookbooks

If you look through the acknowledgments at the beginning of most cookbooks, you will see a grateful mention of the one or more testers who worked on the recipes in the book. This is a job that is becoming increasingly important as cookbook authors become more accurate and precise. Nothing is more aggravating, or potentially embarrassing, than a recipe that just won't work, no matter what you do.

You might think that recipes from talented cooks and chefs would be just fine, with no further need to test them. The fact is that there are so many different ways of talking and writing about food that it is imperative to test recipes. Furthermore, the process of translating a recipe from its spoken form, or from someone else's notes, into a standard, written format is fraught with opportunities to make a mistake. It might be a simple mistake, such as inadvertently substituting *cup* for *teaspoon*. Or it might be that an ingredient is listed in the ingredient list, but then never mentioned in the method for the recipe. Or perhaps the reverse; step five tells you to add the chopped mushrooms, but you don't know how much to add because no measurement is given.

To make sure that the recipes are as foolproof as possible, cookbook authors will frequently hire recipe testers to take a batch of recipes and prepare them. The tester may be paid for materials as well as a per-recipe or per-batch fee. Then, recipe in hand, the tester prepares the dish, following the measurements and methods as literally as possible, and reports on the end result. If questions come up, or the result is inedible, it's back to the drawing board again. To get a good recipe, it may be necessary to test an individual recipe several times, while some may work perfectly the first time.

Usually the cookbook author will try to do some of the testing him- or herself, but this job can be overwhelming, on top of all the other work that goes into preparing a book. This is especially true if the author is a professional chef. Professionals tend to forget the limitations of the home cook; they forget that amateurs don't always have the same tools and ingredients at hand. Professional chefs may develop recipes that involve washing several pots and pans in the course of preparing one single part of a meal, or simmering a sauce for ten to twelve hours to get just the right flavor and texture. These instructions may be too demanding for a home cook with a full-time job and children to look after.

If you know a cookbook author, it might not be so hard to land a job testing recipes. This can be an excellent opportunity for someone who doesn't want to work outside of the home. It does require accuracy and the ability to take careful notes so that you can communicate with the author about the strong or weak points of a recipe. Publishing houses that specialize in cookbooks, or publish a number of cookbooks each year, are another source of information about breaking into this kind of work. Do a little research to locate the senior editor in charge of cookbooks at the publishing house, and write to that person. Explain your abilities and your interest in recipe testing for cookbooks. Another source of information is trade journals. You may find information about an author who is starting work on a book. Try contacting the author by letter to find out about any opportunities. Recipe testing is not the kind of job that is often advertised in the newspapers. You will need to do a little sleuthing to land your first few jobs. Then, once you have established a network, it should become a little easier to find more work in the future.

CHAPTER NINE

Design, Marketing, and Advertising

The list of companies that design, produce, promote, or sell food or food-related items, equipment, and tools is large and growing. In fact, the first time you realize that a whole system of companies is devoted exclusively to promoting and selling food service products, the notion might seem almost unbelievable. Who would ever imagine an advertising agency focused on promoting fresh produce? Or a whole public relations firm, such as the one run by Lisa Ekus, that concentrates all of its energies on cookbooks, restaurants, and a few selected ingredients and cooking tools?

These companies and firms have sprung into existence to fill a particular need—creating a new product, tool, or service, and/or getting the message out to the public that a service or a product exists that can exactly meet their special needs. Sometimes this "public" is the general public that buys food in a grocery store and selects appliances from national chain stores; sometimes it's the "professional public" that makes up the food service industry.

Design Firms

Food service equipment, and restaurants themselves, are constantly being designed, redesigned, and refined to get the best possible results. The people and companies that provide this design service must be able to bring the special needs of their clients to bear on the raw materials they have to work with. These raw materials might be open spaces that need to be turned into a highly efficient Euro-style kitchen for a bistro or a wine glass that must be designed to complement a special decor or showcase a world-renowned wine list with style.

Some design firms specialize in work required by the food service professional: chefs, restaurant and inn owners, dining room managers, and cooks. Others offer their talents to both professionals and the general public. With increased interest in cooking, more and more people are trying to design home kitchens with professional features.

One interesting design and manufacturing company, Best Manufacturer, has turned its attention to hand kitchen tools. This company makes more than forty whisks in several sizes, as well as bean mashers and a special tool used to pop bubbles in pizza doughs so that they will lie perfectly flat as they bake. This company did its homework and found out that most Americans prefer a smooth crust to one that has ballooned and buckled.

All-Clad Manufacturing, Inc., is another company that has devoted extraordinary amounts of research money to developing a series of pots and pans that meet the standards of the most exacting chef. All-Clad's special lines have been developed to avoid such common problems as hot spots due to uneven heat distribution. They also have an interesting new line of cookware that works on induction stoves as well as conventional cooktops.

Designers and manufacturers of large equipment are essential to the smooth operation of any kitchen, and a wide variety of companies are working hard to outfit kitchens of all shapes and sizes. Some will even help with the actual design and layout of a new facility or one that is undergoing a face-lift.

Designing Tools and Equipment

Once people learned to tame fire for their own use, it was not long before they realized that not only did fire provide light and heat, it could also change how food tasted. Of course, nobody knows exactly how long it took for people to begin the process of learning to cook, but we can speculate on what course the evolution might have taken.

Over time, people learned to raise a variety of foods, including grains. Animals were domesticated and raised as well. The next logical step was to produce a variety of pots, racks, and other cooking utensils to handle these foods. First, pouches of skin might have been used to hold water so that grains could be boiled. Eventually, pots of clay and then metal made it a much simpler matter to boils meats, vegetables, and grains.

Some of the advances made—learning to make leavened breads, cheeses, and discovering which foods were edible—are so important that it is almost impossible to imagine what would happen if the accumulated knowledge of thousands of years should be lost overnight. One wonders how the first person to taste cheese or beer reacted, and where the courage to try something so foreign to the tongue came from.

The quest for knowledge in the culinary arts continues today. Development of tools and other pieces of equipment that suit the needs of the contemporary kitchen is an important, thriving industry. The range of tools and equipment being redesigned, refined, or invented includes everything from large pieces, such as refrigeration units and stoves, to small items, such as paper goods that will keep take-out food at the proper temperature without leaking or littering the earth for the next three hundred years.

Today, design specialists and cooks alike continue to search for better-built cooking utensils such as:

- Knives that hold their edges longer, stay sharper, last longer, have a better balance in the hand

- Pots that are nonstick and durable, enabling chefs to cook foods with less and less added fat

- Scales that are increasingly accurate

- Stoves that are more efficient in their use of fuel, that fit more exactly the needs of a special kitchen task

- Equipment that chops, purees, freezes, and manipulates foods in dozens of ways previously possible only through hours of tedious labor

Of all the new pieces of equipment, tools, and gadgets coming into use in the modern kitchen, the one tool with the most versatility is probably the computer. Computers are coming into the kitchen not only to streamline inventory, costing, and scheduling chores, but also to allow the chef to experiment with foods, reduce or multiply recipes, develop new recipes, adjust existing recipes, and refine techniques rapidly and efficiently. The software available to the chef today affords the chance to customize foods to meet specific nutritional goals, costing needs, or any other specification the chef may have in mind.

Computers and their supporting software have had enormous impact on nutrient analysis. There is no longer any doubt that nutritional cooking is here to stay. Daily, stories appear in magazines and newspapers, giving people new information about the importance of the food they eat. As Americans become more concerned with fitness and with adjusting their lifestyles to meet the demands of our present-day society, they are demanding food that is more nutritious, without any noticeable sacrifice of the flavor and richness they have come to expect as the norm.

The computer equipment and software developed for use in the professional kitchen are only as good as the people designing them. More and more often, these computer professionals are people with culinary backgrounds.

Advertising Agencies

Restaurants, hotels, chains, and distributors all need to advertise themselves to the public. The growth of advertising and public relations firms that deal exclusively with food is a recent phenomenon, but one that clearly indicates the importance, and economic value, of the culinary arts. These specialized agencies need people skilled in the culinary arts to make sure that the right message is getting out to the right market.

One of the largest international public relations and advertising agencies is Ketchum. It handles a vast number of accounts of all sorts. One woman has achieved great success working for Ketchum as the director of food promotion and recipe development division. Maggie Waldron came to this work after spending her childhood living in hotels. Her father was a hotelier, and she went on to study hotel management at Cornell University. Although she had her heart set on becoming a chef, she found that the climate was unfriendly toward women chefs when she graduated. Her life became a mosaic of different experiences, including work as a food stylist for *McCall's*, one of the first magazines to consider food photography an artistic exercise. From there she went to Europe, where she learned more about food, cooking, and art. Eventually, she found herself living in San Francisco, doing food styling assignments out of her kitchen. Shortly thereafter, she was recruited by Ketchum, and a state-of-the-art test kitchen was constructed so that she could do her job.

Today, Maggie Waldron is credited with the advertising campaigns that gave a new image to raisins (for the California Raisin Advisory Council), gave potatoes a new, less fattening reputation (for the Potato Board), and promoted trimmed-down beef (for the Beef Industry Council).

As you can see, this kind of work doesn't just fall into your lap without any effort on your part. It takes a great deal of time, patience, and perseverance to arrive at the heights reached by Maggie Waldron. However, there is a distinct lesson to be learned. Throughout her studies and her life experiences, she was able to keep a focus on what she really wanted to do.

A number of agencies handle advertising for the various councils, special interest groups, and companies that need to develop a strong ad campaign to introduce a new product or to enhance the image of an established item. A great many skills go into developing such a campaign. And the range of services offered by public relations firms specializing in the hospitality industry has become incredibly diversified.

Consider Lisa Ekus's firm. In addition to preparing press releases announcing the publication of a new cookbook, it will arrange nationwide tours including interviews with the press, radio, and television. The firm plans in-store demonstrations and organizes special seminars to train chefs and authors to promote their books successfully. These seminars stress both public speaking skills and the special techniques used to present a few recipes from the book as part of a demonstration.

Other agencies, such as the Plummer Group, can create entire menu or restaurant concepts for a client. Still others, such as Noble Tennant, undertake everything from recipe development to the publication of newsletters. These firms may also be able to provide access to special research or prepare still photography or demonstration videotapes to help promote the client's product.

These companies look for staff members with writing skills, the ability to communicate effectively and appropriately, a good grasp of market potential, and the wisdom to select a good variety of approaches to selling an item. The contemporary advertiser must be able to discuss print media, photography, videos, television, and radio advertising fluently. Successful promotion efforts today seldom concentrate on one avenue or medium to the exclusion of all others.

To develop skill in these diverse media, it is essential to gain as much experience as possible, in whatever ways you can. You can take one or more courses in a particular area. You will probably find yourself working at an entry-level capacity, and you may find that you can volunteer to help out with the photo sessions, editing sessions, or taping sessions to get an idea of what goes on. Training sessions may require the special skills a former teacher or actor might bring to this field. Testing and recipe development demand cooking skills. This is not an avenue for shrinking violets. You do have to promote yourself and gain as many skills as possible before anyone is likely to entrust you with a multimillion-dollar account.

Consultation

Consultation can cover a fairly wide gamut. It may mean that you will be hired by a restaurant to review a menu and assist in giving it a face-lift, or even major surgery. You may be hired by an individual to help get a new diet off and running. Or a corporate dining facility may need some help training employees to prepare new menu items.

Companies that develop or manufacture cooking equipment often look for individuals to help demonstrate their wares at shows and other events throughout the country. Your responsibility may be nothing greater than to show up on time and run through a prepared script, or you may be looked to for guidance. You may develop recipes to demonstrate the equipment to its best advantage and perhaps even produce a small pamphlet or training video to help the company promote its product.

Once again, these positions are not likely to be found in the help-wanted section of the newspaper listed under *cook* or *chef*. But a little research on your part, keeping informed and abreast of new models of equipment developed for both consumer and professional use, will start to give you a sense of who might be in the market for this type of consulting service. Going to trade shows will also be a help.

Private Consultation Services

Chet Holden left his work at a noted public relations and advertising agency that specialized in food service accounts. He wanted to make a go of it on his own. From the early days when he spent hours on the telephone and prepared countless proposals in the little alcove in his family room, he has emerged to find himself busier than he had ever dreamed possible, doing things that would have sounded crazy even a year or two ago.

Chet provides some very special services for his clients. He breaks his business into three categories. He writes and edits for companies, helping them with ad copy, newsletters, scripts for videos, and direct mailings. He also does product and recipe development. And he offers industry training workshops. One seminar he recalled with great emotion called for him to spend eight straight hours with a very special sales staff. A major food producer hires chefs to do all of its sales. Chet was brought in to work with them on conceptual creativity and menu development. He recalled how hard it was to imagine talking about flavor principles, brainstorming, and ideational skills. But he did his research at home and in the university library in his hometown, prepared a curriculum, did whatever else he could to get ready, and then off he flew to meet with his students.

Other individuals may take on less ambitious projects. A local pizza shop may want a little help with its menu. Maybe the owners want to jazz it up with a few ethnic or healthy dishes. Or maybe they just want a little help training or motivating their staff. It is very possible to turn a pet interest into a valuable, salable commodity. It will take additional research to discover ways to market yourself and the service or product you offer. And you must be prepared to allow plenty of time for your business to grow. But there is no reason to think that your "far-fetched" idea won't work.

Direct and Mail-Order Sales

You've probably seen the small ads in local "shoppers," newspapers, and even magazines that are distributed nationwide. They read more or less like this:

> *Fabulous cheesecake! Send for foolproof recipe, enclosing $1 shipping/handling and long SASE to John Baker, 11 Main Street, Smalltown, USA 54301.*

Even if you've never sent for a recipe yourself, plenty of other people do. The cost of this type of work is surprisingly small. You just place a two- or three-line classified ad in the paper or magazine of your choice, get a recipe of yours copied several times, and there you are. Today, you might even consider faxing recipes hither and yon. There are several interesting, attractive options for someone with a catchy, wonderful recipe.

This works for more than recipes, too. A local sales paper, the *PennySaver*, recently had two different ads offering special products. One was for handmade fudge, shipped anywhere in one-, two-, or five-pound blocks. Another was for home-baked muffins, also available to ship anywhere throughout the nation.

A small company that blends specialty teas, the Gertrude Ford Company was approached by a mail-order company to acquire sole distribution rights through the mail. The company also advertised locally for a person to handle processing the orders to make sure that the tea company knew how much tea to ship and where it was to go. This job was filled by an eager young woman with a personal computer, a printer, and a modem. Other mail-order companies specializing in foods and cookware offer similar work to individuals in their homes.

CHAPTER TEN

Media and Communication

There is an aura of glamour associated with being a food photographer, stylist, or writer. Professionals in these fascinating careers rarely follow a common path. There is one uniting thread, however, and that is a certain fascination with food—the ways that it can be described, prepared, served, viewed, enjoyed, and even eaten.

Food writers, critics, essayists, and historians form a special cadre of food service professionals. We will look at a number of well-known authors, photographers, stylists, and others who work in the literary and artistic side of the food service business. Photographers and graphic artists are involved in the visual display of foods. Not every photograph of food can qualify as fine art, and not every restaurant review can be considered great literature, but there is always the potential for excellence. Some very special talents are required to translate something as sensual, tactile, and aromatic as food into typewritten words and graphic images.

Magazines, advertisements, videos, and photographs of or about food are of seemingly endless interest to the American public. But these articles and images are only successful when they reflect the expertise of their creators. If the public is confident that the person who is writing about a restaurant could actually cook a meal, or that the video about preparing fish has been produced by someone who truly understands the subject, then it works. The most successful projects have someone involved who can cook and who loves food.

Food Photographers

Have you ever picked up a magazine or a book because the food on the front cover looked so appealing that you wanted to eat it? It takes someone with a very special talent to produce pictures of such breathtaking beauty and style. It isn't always easy to make food look appealing in a photograph.

Capturing the true colors, keeping the background perfectly balanced so that the primary image isn't lost or overwhelmed, and selecting the right filter so that the texture comes through are just a few of the difficulties the photographer faces. But when the perfect lighting, the exact f-stop, and the correct depth of field are captured in a photograph, a miracle can happen. Instead of a flat picture, the food seems to have all of the flavor, texture, and color you would see if you were right there next to it. Think of the homey photos of the last fantastic family picnic or outdoor barbecue you attended. While you were there, you saw everything as inviting and delicious. But when the snapshots get placed in the family album, it just looks like a big jumble of stuff.

The professional food photographer knows the problems that can crop up along the way to achieving a picture that looks good enough to eat. When the food is sitting right in front of you, your sense of smell and taste influence how appealing (or unappealing) you find it. You can experience the different textures, the temperature, the thickness, the spiciness—all of the important elements. But with photography, you have only your vision to go on. This means that the way the food looks has to be enhanced to the utmost with every trick in the photographer's bag. Certain lenses, lights, or filters may give the food a particular appearance, making it more or less muddy or bright. Filling the frame, or keeping plenty of space around the subject, may also enhance (or detract from) the way that we will experience the finished photograph.

Some foods are not visually appealing. But the challenge is somehow to make them look that way, whether for an ad campaign, a feature story in a magazine, or the jacket of a new cookbook.

No schools really specialize in food photography, although there are many special courses you can take. It is important to understand the basic principles of photography and lighting, how to operate a camera, and how to arrange foods so that they look appealing.

Food photographers may work independently as freelancers, or they may be part of the permanent staff of an institution, magazine, or publishing house. John Grubell and his assistant, Loma Smith, are staff members at a prestigious cooking school in the Northeast. Their work is varied, to say the least. One day may find them working on "plated shots," where finished dishes are prepared and arranged as they might be served to a guest. On another day they will be doing a series of "ID shots" to showcase a number of different food items. These two photographers don't always have a stylist or even a gofer to gather the thousand and one props that a shot might require. This means that sometimes they will have to dig up just the right tablecloth, plate, glass, or other element to complete the picture. They also may have to fill out requisitions to the storeroom for foods or travel to nearby shops to find just the right product if it isn't available in any of the school's kitchens. Some days a chef is on hand to prepare and arrange the foods, and other days the photographers will either do it themselves or rely upon one of the in-house editors for assistance.

John and Loma must be able to work with a number of different cameras and in different formats: 35 millimeter, 2¼, 4 x 5, black and white, color, slides, prints, and digital. While they send their film out to independent laboratories for developing and printing, other photographers prefer to maintain their own darkrooms so that they have even greater control over the finished product.

The ability to use digital cameras and imaging software is an increasingly important part of the photographer's craft. These images can be used on websites, for PowerPoint presentations, or other applications.

Photographers like Franz Mitterer and Roger Kramer, who both work for the international hardcover magazine, *Art Culinaire*, have continually pushed the boundaries of what can be done in food photography. Their imaginative, unusual use of special lighting techniques has changed the way that other photographers approach their work. Freelance photographers who do work for catalogs, calendars, advertisements, and cookbooks are changing the style of their work, too, reflecting a growing sophistication about all things culinary. Maria Robdelo is a Colombian-born food photographer whose work has had a strong impact in the field. Ben Fink, a New York–based photographer specializing in food, has contributed enormously to the success of the projects with which he has been involved, including *Artisan Baking* and *The Professional Chef* (Seventh Edition).

Graphic artists and illustrators are also in demand. Cookbooks need cover and interior designs. Food shows up on posters, labels, packaging, and a whole host of other items that are directly handled by illustrators and graphic artists. Gary Allen, an illustrator based in Woodstock, New York, uses his computer to create the designs for many of the projects he is commissioned to do.

Food Stylists

Preparing the food and placing or arranging it is often the work of a second person who works hand in glove with the photographer. This person is known as a food stylist. When you look at a magazine article and are struck by the way the food is presented, the way it is garnished, or the presence or lack of other props, such as special linens, fresh flowers, baskets, or bottles of wine, in the photography, you are admiring the work of the food stylist.

Stylists, like food photographers, usually undergo a primarily on-the-job training. A few courses are offered, but, in general, it is not something in which you can major at college.

It is up to the stylist to make sure that the lettuce leaves are crisp and crunchy looking and that the sauce is carefully ladled onto the plate (and not on the rim). Stylists check for lint, thumbprints, or traces of grease on glasses, flatware, or plates that might detract from the image. They also make certain that the strawberry is turned the right way, that there are no stray elements that sneak into the picture. They check constantly to be sure that what should be seen is immediately visible and that what shouldn't be seen stays invisible.

Without some knowledge of food—how to select the best product and apply the right technique, how to cut the vegetables and slice the turkey—the stylist would be at a loss.

Delores Custer, a well-known food stylist based in New York City, has gained an enormous reputation for her ability to make a bowl of soup or a basket of fruit come alive for the camera.

She now teaches her craft at various schools throughout New York State, helping her students understand the tricks of the stylist. She patiently introduces them to the unlikely looking tools of the trade that belong in the stylist's kit: tweezers, hair dryers, irons, pieces of foam, funnels, cotton swabs and balls, spray bottles, and paintbrushes.

As her students discover, you may have to sort through a bushel of apples to find just the right one for a photograph. She also reminds them that fashions in food styling change dramatically from year to year, influenced by television, movies, and the latest trend in clothing and interior design, as well as by the work that the hottest chefs are doing in restaurants around the world. The picture-perfect shiny red apple with nary a dent or scrape of yesterday has given way to a more earthy, organically raised version today, with an intriguing scar or blemish, a bit of twig or a slightly wilted leaf still attached to the fruit.

Television and Videos

Instructional television shows about cooking really got started in a big way when Julia Child had such enormous success with her PBS series, "The French Chef." Today, local access channels and PBS boast numerous shows—from nationally syndicated ones such as Jeff Smith as "The Frugal Gourmet" to local interest shows that limit their audiences to a single city. And you needn't necessarily appear on camera; the audience never sees Marian Marsh, the culinary curator for the PBS series "Victory Garden."

Videos have made dramatic impact on the way cooking is taught today. Many new cookbooks feature a series of videos as part of the package, or they at least offer a short demonstration tape to give potential buyers a preview of the book. Videos that teach basic and advanced culinary techniques have really come into their own. Henry Woods, director of the Learning Resources Center at the Culinary Institute of America, says that he has witnessed a boom in interest among both professional chefs and home cooks. He has a wonderfully talented staff working under his direction to prepare scripts; operate cameras; create the necessary graphics; edit the film; and handle marketing, sales, and distribution of the school's instructional tapes. Henry brings to his work a very special affinity for the subject matter. Before beginning his work for the school, he attended it as a student, graduating in 1978. His experience with cooking and his love for food form the invaluable foundation for his work, along with a keen, personal awareness of how best to take advantage of all that video offers as a teaching tool.

There is a great deal of support work that goes into any video or television project, and it takes many more hands than those of the star. Recipes are researched and tested. Preparations are put through a dry run. Timing and support during the taping or filming is usually in the hands of the cooks and stylists who are never seen on camera. Someone who has the organizational skills it takes to keep a film or video project on time, on budget, and up to the standards of the director or producer is very much in demand.

If you are just getting started in the culinary arts, you may not be asked to star in a show, but you may be able to get your feet in the door in a number of different ways. You can be a minion, chopping vegetables, dashing to the flower shop or the grocery store, sorting through box after box of mushrooms to find the perfect size or shape, and setting up *mise en place* and "swaps" for the chef to use during the taping. (*Swap* refers to having a dish already prepared to a specific point, so that the show doesn't grind to a halt while you wait for the turkey to roast or the veal shank to braise.)

Writing

All you have to do is walk into any bookstore to see that there is a large, and seemingly inexhaustible, market for cookbooks. They range from single-subject books on anything from beans to chocolate to books that center on a particular type of cuisine or ethnic style. Some books are encyclopedic in their scope. The people who write, edit, and sell these books have to have a good basic knowledge of food and cooking in order for these books to work.

The way to break into food writing is simply to write as much as you can and try to get it published wherever you can. Small local papers are always looking for someone to write for them; the catch is that they will probably not pay much, if they can pay anything at all. You have to pay your dues if you want to break into this field. You will have the chance to have your work published, though.

Another way to get some experience is to help with organizations that want to put together small cookbooks as a part of a money-raising project. Junior league books are increasingly sophisticated, as are other cookbooks sponsored by church and town organizations. The practice of writing and editing recipes can be invaluable. If nothing else, you will find out immediately if this is something that you can do on a daily basis.

Being able to hold a piece in your hand that you have written or helped to write is the same thing as holding a diploma. It can take a long time to get to that point, however, so don't get discouraged if you truly want to write about food. And keep your day job!

Books

Writing books is just one avenue for the person who wants to write about food. But it is certainly the one that most often comes to mind first when someone loves both writing and food. The subjects that are fodder for cookbooks and books about food are staggering. Food historians such as Margaret Visser, Elizabeth David, and Waverly Root have written some masterpieces. Margaret Visser, for example, was a classicist by training and a self-described "anthropologist of everyday life." She is the author of *Much Depends on Dinner*, an entertaining and delightful look at what eating habits and manners say about societies and their cultures. Calvin Trillin, another intriguing author, has been writing for the *New Yorker* since 1963. Along the way, he has found that writing about food has been one of the great joys of his career. He too has taken time out to write a few wonderful books, such as *Alice, Let's Eat*.

Traditional cookbooks, full of recipes and information about cooking, are a vast and growing part of the publishing industry. Producing these books involves a whole army of people. The author might be the chef or cook whose recipe collection is featured. Or there may be a ghost writer such as Peter Frumkin, who wrote the text for Claude Guermond, chef of La Pavilion and author of *The Norman Table*. Yet another scenario is that used by Time-Life, which gathered together a number of well-known food writers and authorities, including M. F. K. Fisher, Julia Child, Richard Olney, and Craig Claiborne, to prepare and edit its highly successful cookbook series.

Individual authors will probably need a literary agent. Some agents or agencies specialize strictly in cookbooks. And there is usually an in-house editor at most major publishing houses who handles cookbooks and related topics. Pam Chirls, senior editor at Van Nostrand Reinhold, works in the hospitality division of her publishing company, producing books about food, hotel and restaurant management, and other topics. Each project requires other specialists, including copyeditors and production managers and marketing and sales personnel, all of whom contribute a particular expertise to the project.

Feature Articles

Most magazines and newspapers have a core staff that prepares the majority of the articles as well as the standard columns featured in any issue. But there are usually a number of contributing editors and freelance writers who develop an idea for a story, write it, and then pitch it to the food editor. The more often you can get your name in print in a magazine or newspaper, the better your chances of continuing to find work. Nao Hauser, a food writer and editor, spends the time between work on major books by combining food and travel writing for *Bon Appétit* and *Food & Wine*.

There are a number of trade and consumer publications that focus on food, and many newspapers devote a portion of their papers (usually on Wednesday) to food and entertainment. The person who writes these articles is usually well read in the culinary arts and proficient in the kitchen as well. The kinds of articles that might be called for could range from a simple discussion of how to brew a pot of tea to an informational piece on nutritional cooking or special new foods.

Restaurant Reviews

Restaurant critics are important to both restaurants and diners. Critics are notorious for their highly personalized opinions, but it is interesting to note just how influential some critics can be. Bryan Miller, former food critic for the *New York Times*, and Phyllis Richman of the *Washington Post* are two of the most well-known critics in the nation. This kind of writing job is not easy to come by, and people who hold these highly coveted positions often cultivate an air of glamour and mystery. Fundamentally, however, a reviewer who wants to be taken seriously needs a solid grounding in what constitutes both good food and good cooking. In addition, he or she should be able to discuss the wine list, the style of the restaurant, and trends in the restaurant business.

Reviews of cookbooks, small pieces on new foods or equipment, human interest stories, press releases—all of these are examples of the kinds of pieces that you may be able to pitch to magazines to start your portfolio. Read the publications, both trade and consumer, to understand their audiences. Then study the publishing process. There are publications that explain how to submit articles to magazines for consideration.

Writing for the Web

The Web is a powerful tool for everyone in business today. Guests and clients have come to expect that they will find all sorts of information and services there. Someone has to actually put together the content, check it carefully, and manage it. There are a variety of relatively new outlets for writers willing to work in this electronic environment. There are some sites that need articles or essays, short descriptions for how-to sequences, advertising copy, or recipes. They, like magazines, have a specific audience in mind. Some sites are for professionals, some for members of a very particular group, others for a general audience, still others for niche audiences such as those with specific food allergies.

Bookstores and Libraries

If you love to read about cooking and cuisine, but you aren't interested in working in a restaurant, running a catering company, or writing or editing a book or syndicated column, what do you do? Well, if you are Nach Waxman, you open one of the best known bookstores in the United States, Kitchen Arts & Letters, stock it with between six and seven thousand titles dealing strictly with food and wine, and then wait for the customers to come through the door. And they do. Mr. Waxman says he loves to dispense conversation and information along with the books he sells. There are other bookstores with a similar single-subject slant throughout the country, including Cook's Library, owned by Ellen Rose, with nearly three thousand titles, and JB Prince Co. of New York, a mail-order distributor of around two hundred titles to professional chefs.

Professional librarians can also indulge a passion for gastronomy by trying to land a job in one of the many special libraries devoted to food, cooking, and wine. The New York City Public Library boasts an impressive collection devoted to food. The Katherine Angell Library is another gold mine for food writers, historians, and students; it is housed in Roth Hall at the Culinary Institute of America. Other universities and schools, as well as private foundations, may also have large or small collections of interesting, rare, and unusual books on cooking.

Consumer Advocacy
Groups and Food Lobbyists

Not everyone who is involved in writing, filming, or photographing food is part of the public media. Advocacy groups are concerned with advancing consumer rights and food safety in a whole range of areas. The issues that they deal with may range from concerns about the safety of whole eggs and their relation to salmonella outbreaks to answering fears about food irradiation. One of these groups, Americans for Safe Food, Center for Science in the Public Interest, has a newsletter and has recently published a book called *Safe Food*.

In the same vein, but approaching the issue from another perspective, are the environmental resource groups such as the Land Institute or the Natural Resources Defense Council. These organizations hope to learn more about food and have a direct influence on the way that it is raised, packaged, distributed, and ultimately disposed of. Their work is aimed at preventing the ecological imbalance that occurs when we repeatedly take from the land without being concerned about conserving all natural resources, replenishing renewable resources, and keeping the environment wholesome and safe for our own and future generations. The Land Institute, for example, conducts research into the development of viable, ecologically sound alternatives to standard agricultural practices. Its primary interest is how plants interrelate as part of a natural ecosystem. Its members feel this knowledge could be developed to enhance growth of a variety of foods without relying on chemical pesticides, herbicides, and fertilizers. The work done by these groups brings together a number of specialists from various fields: people knowledgeable about food, agriculture, and ecology, as well as lawyers, scientists, and environmentalists.

Lobbyists

Food lobbyists working in Washington, D.C., are registered as lobbying for the food industry in the *Washington Representative*. These groups are responsible for promoting the special legislative needs of general food companies, institutes, and associations. Examples include the Future Farmers of America, National American Wholesale Grocers' Association, and International Apple Institute. Some of the groups listed as consumer advocacy groups are also registered lobbyists; Center for Science in the Public Interest is one such organization. In addition to these general interest groups, companies that market a specific product or commodity may also be represented by registered lobbyists. The primary intention of any lobbyist is to enlist the support of as many members of the House of Representatives and the Senate as possible. Numerous laws and resolutions are passed each session that may have a vast impact on the way these groups conduct business.

The skills required by lobbying groups are often very particular. Most of these positions require a minimum of four years of college. Experience in politics is indispensable for those interested in working as lobbyists, and a thorough knowledge of the needs and concerns of the group they represent is equally important. Some specialists go on to obtain doctorates in their respective fields. However, there is plenty of work to be done by those who are still in training or by those who simply want to become professional lobbyists.

CHAPTER ELEVEN

Finding and Landing a Job

D reams are fine, but if all you do is dream about a career, then nothing much will happen. Getting the right education is an excellent beginning, but it is no guarantee that a world-famous chef from a five-star restaurant will beg you to come work as a sous-chef.

It will take some hard thought and some careful preparation to get a good job, and it may take several tries before you land the right job. This chapter is a brief introduction to finding your way when you start to look for a job.

Choosing a Direction

As you have seen throughout this book, the number of options available in the culinary arts is nothing short of overwhelming. Deciding which path to take can be equally overwhelming. But there are some ways to at least narrow the number of directions that are suitable for you.

First of all, be as honest as you can in answering some of the following questions.

1. Do you really want to spend most of your time cooking?

A love of food can translate into a love of cooking, but it doesn't always. A great many people find enormous satisfaction in preparing food for others. But an equally great number would rather express themselves differently.

Working in a kitchen can be exciting and exhilarating for some people. The challenge of getting everything ready on time, meeting deadlines, and working quickly to the top of their potential is a thrill. Without that kind of adrenaline rush, they would find their lives lacking in something. It isn't unusual to find an executive chef who spends most days in an office filling out forms and dealing with administrative problems—and champing at the bit to get back on the line, even if it's just for few hours during the busy part of service.

Others don't want the kind of daily stress that comes with a job in a restaurant or hotel kitchen. There are plenty of other places to look for work without leaving the culinary arts. There is administration, writing about food, working for a company in research and development, or consulting, to name just a few alternatives.

2. Is it important to you to be in charge?

Not everyone in this field winds up as an executive chef in charge of a hotel or a superstar chef who gets written up in the newspaper. Someone has to work the line, butcher the meats, and perform the countless necessary jobs of any food service operation, from the smallest restaurant to the largest hotel chain. And a great many people simply aren't interested in going beyond a certain level.

There is no excuse for stopping short of your own potential through simple laziness, but there is also no point in spending a lifetime berating yourself for not reaching the top of the heap if you never really wanted to be there in the first place.

3. How well do you relate to, or work with, the public?

Even though the chef is often hidden away in the kitchen, safe from the eyes of the public, he or she is not immune to demands, criticisms, or compliments on the food and its presentation. If you are uncomfortable with the idea of a great many people passing judgement on your work, or with meeting the demands of your customers, you probably will want to work in an area of the culinary arts where you will be less visible.

If you thrive on the give-and-take of dealing with people, you may prefer to move out of the "back of the house" into a position where you can be in more constant contact.

4. How important is it to you to be able to spend "normal" hours with your family and friends?

The "normal" hours for a great many people in the restaurant industry are far from what others consider normal. You don't have to seek a different job simply to spend Sunday and Thanksgiving at home. However, you will probably want to consider working for schools, corporations, or other organizations that can offer the average nine-to-five, Monday-through-Friday schedule. These positions are available.

Many people find that working hours when the rest of the world is at play, and relaxing when everyone else is at work, has its own built-in bonus. Lines at the bank and supermarket are shorter, restaurants are less crowded, and appointments at the dentist are easier to arrange.

Before you settle on a schedule, recognize whether you are an incurable night owl or early bird. Then decide how willing you are to try to fight your night-owl tendencies before you take a job working in a bakeshop from 4 A.M. to 2 P.M. It may be incredibly difficult when you truly prefer to get up at noon, go to work at 3 P.M., and work until midnight.

5. How much money do you want to make?

Working in the food service industry is one way to be sure that you are never out of work. People will always eat, and you will always have some sort of job—whether it's making salads in a school cafeteria or cooking burgers in a fast-food restaurant. Admittedly, these jobs will not make you rich quickly, but they are "safe."

The really high salaries that you may have heard about and longed for are usually secured by those people who are willing to take a risk on a new business or who advance to demanding positions. Finding the right combination of circumstances does play a part. For the most part, however, your salary is determined quite simply by how willing you are to work, how interested you are in your job, and how motivated you are to try new things, either on your own or at work.

Salaries are determined to some extent by where you live. Those in northeastern states, for example, will usually have higher salaries than those in southern states. Normally, places that offer higher salaries also have a much higher cost of living. Be sure to take that into consideration. A salary that would allow you to live like a king in West Virginia might not be enough to keep you in food and bus fare in New York City or San Francisco.

Finding a Job

There are many different sources you can turn to when you are looking for a job, whether it is your first job or the next move on your personal career ladder. The obvious and time-honored place to look is the classified ads in a local newspaper. Many newspapers provide their classified ads on-line, and it is easier than ever before to research work in a new community, if relocation is your aim. There are a host of reputable websites devoted to job searches that help with resume posting and screening services. Be sure to take the time to get to know something about your source. Different types of employers tend to use different types of listing services.

In addition to the classified ads, you can do your own survey of establishments where you think you'd like to work. Get to know what they do and what kind of employees they have. Now try to come up with a job description for yourself, if you worked for them. Try to answer the question employers like to ask any potential candidate: what can you do for me? Write this up as a proposal, send it to the employer along with some support for your claims (letters of reference, a resume, or similar items).

Agencies and headhunters can help you find jobs that aren't listed in the classifieds, but they may require a fee, either up front paid by you or as a commission paid either by you or your employer.

One of the single most effective ways to find your dream job is word of mouth. In order to cash in on what the grapevine is buzzing about, you have to be plugged in. This is where networking really pays off.

Networking

The best jobs are not usually advertised in the papers. You find out about them through the grapevine. Establishing a network within the industry is essential. You can look to the members of your network for all sorts of valuable help. You may hear about business opportunities, new food sources, or special events of particular interest. As an employer, you may find it easier to locate the right person to fill a job.

The way to begin a network is to introduce yourself to others in the industry. Have business cards printed and use them. If you are in a restaurant on a night that is not extremely busy, ask your waiter if you can meet the chef. Attend local, regional, and national shows. The schedules for these shows are usually available from organizations such as the National Restaurant Association and the American Culinary Federation.

Read trade journals, and if something strikes a chord, send a letter to the person who wrote the article. Cooking schools and cooking classes are another natural way to meet other people who share your interest. The school may have an alumni organization, making it that much easier to contact people throughout the country. There are a number of different ways to set up networks. Once you have begun, it gets increasingly easier. Resumes, cover letters, phone calls, and networking are essential tools that will help you get on your way.

Food service is a growing industry, one that shows no signs of slowing significantly. Today there is room for a wider variety of people, doing a wider variety of jobs, than ever before. You are lucky to have chosen this path.

Interviewing for a Job

The first task of any job is getting the job. To do that, you must get an interview. In order to attract the interest of a potential employer, you can:

- Write a cover letter and include a resume

- Call on the telephone

- Drop by the restaurant or business

Any of these methods can work, depending upon the type of job for which you are applying and the style of the operation.

Try to learn as much as you can about the operation before sending a cover letter or making a call. Find out the name of the chef, the manager, the owner, or anyone who holds a position of power. Newspaper or magazine articles might include this information. You might also be able to find out by calling the personnel director. If the operation is too small to have a personnel director, ask whoever answers the phone.

If you want a job in a restaurant, try to get a look at a menu to find out what type of food the restaurant serves. If possible, have a meal there. Observe the style of service, note the hours and how busy it is. Ask questions of the wait staff, too. They can often furnish information that you might not get otherwise. Getting all of this information will take at least a little sleuthing on your part. This is as true of advertising agencies as it is of restaurants. The point is this: the more effort you make to find out as much as you can about a potential job, the better it will reflect on you during the interview.

When you arrive for the interview, remember what kind of position you are applying for and dress accordingly. If you want to work in the kitchen, a coat and tie is nice but not essential. However, if your intention is to work as the dining room manager, dress as you would for work. No matter what kind of position you want, be sure that you are neatly dressed and well groomed. Kitchen workers usually have hands that look as if they are no strangers to hard work, but they shouldn't look as if they have never had a run-in with soap and a nailbrush.

Be on time. Your interview sets the stage for almost everything that comes later. Punctuality is essential in the food service industry.

The style of the interview will be determined in part by the size of the operation, and in part by the personality of the interviewer. Be sure to have your resume with you. It could help you in filling out any necessary forms, and it shows a professional attitude.

Interview Questions

Answer questions as well and as truthfully as you can. At times you may wonder if you are being asked a "trick question." Keep in mind that an overall confidence about your skills and an ability to listen can tip the scales in your favor, more than any specific answers. Your experience and education both come into play. Don't be discouraged if you draw a blank at first. Slow down a little, concentrate, and do the best you can. Interviews make everyone nervous.

Typical Interview Questions

1. Where do you want to be in five, ten, or fifteen years?

2. What steps are you willing to take to reach your goals? What steps have you already taken?

3. What do you expect to achieve on this job?

4. Why have you chosen the culinary arts as a profession?

5. What can you contribute to this company?

6. What motivates you to work your hardest and reach your goals?

7. What makes something a success or a failure? How do you react to either?

8. What qualities do you have that would make you a good candidate for this position?

9. How would you describe yourself?

10. What salary are you expecting?

When the interview is over, ask when you can expect to hear something about the job. Sending a note is a good way to emphasize your interest. Thank the person who gave you the interview. Then, if you are not contacted in a reasonable amount of time, call back to ask about the status of your application.

CHAPTER TWELVE

Making Your Own Path

Writing a Business Plan

No matter how big or small your business is, you need to write a business plan. A business plan helps you to define your objectives, identify your market, analyze your competition, develop appropriate advertising and public relations strategies, do a budget and a forecast, and much more.

Every business benefits from a clear focus, whether you are planning a brand new convention center/golf course or a mail-order business selling premixed spice blends from your home kitchen. One major benefit of writing it all down is that it keeps you from getting distracted or wasting your two most precious commodities, time and money.

In addition, funding for your business is easier to win if lenders can see that you have done the necessary legwork to determine how to run a business, when it will show a profit, and how much business you can reasonably expect, based upon your services and the clientele you intend to serve.

There are software packages available to help you write a business plan, as well as seminars and workshops devoted to the subject. Taking the time to write, rewrite, and tailor your business plan until it has a custom fit pays off from the moment you take action and every moment thereafter.

A business plan, like a resume, benefits from periodic review and update. If you've been in business for some time, you may have strayed from your original plan. Perhaps you need to streamline, or perhaps you need to incorporate your new activities into the plan.

Set specific goals—expressed in terms of productivity, new ventures to plan or undertake, budget goals, and financial goals—at regular intervals.

As part of your business plan, be sure to write a succinct job description for yourself and every other member of the team. Keep these descriptions up-to-date. Have backup plans to account for worst-case scenarios and strategies for common problems. Write these plans down, too, and keep them close at hand as a resource and a guide.

Set schedules and deadlines for yourself. Use them as a yardstick to measure your progress and keep you from digressing. A specific time frame does a lot to keep your dreams and schemes from vaporizing into mist.

Putting Your Plan into Action

The world has experienced enormous changes as we moved from hunting and gathering to agriculture and, finally, into an industrially driven economy. Once again, we are facing a major upheaval as our economy becomes less industrial and more service oriented. We are just starting to understand what this means in terms of job opportunities for the creative and dynamic people in the food service industry.

One of the possibilities that is just starting to take hold is the notion of providing a very specialized service to meet the needs of a carefully identified group. There is a great deal of challenge and satisfaction in taking the germ of an idea and beginning a business.

More people than ever before are turning on their home computers, plugging in their fax machines, and letting their imaginations take charge as they plot a whole new course for themselves.

Some of these cottage industries require very specialized education. Others are the brainchild of a moment's inspiration (or even desperation) as a person takes a good hard look at daily life and says, "There must be a better, easier way—and I bet I could make money from the answer!"

Keeping Your Skills Sharp

For every service that you offer, think about ways that you might improve that service. This will point out to you any special skills, training, degrees, equipment, or support services you might need. For example, if you provide nutritional or dietary advice and counseling as part of your services, you need to remember that no matter what degree you got, or where you got it, your area of expertise—nutrition in this case—is changing and evolving all the time.

Continuing education in the form of reading, course work, additional degrees, fieldwork, or research may be necessary to stay current. If all your clients are clamoring for the Zone or the Atkins plans, you need to know about those diets. If a client comes to you because his or her doctor has prescribed a low-cholesterol diet to cope with a form of coronary disease or a macrobiotic diet to assist in a holistic approach to cancer treatment, you need to understand not only the parameters of the diet but the specifics of the condition you are being asked to help with.

Consultants who offer clients advice on menus, staffing, training, or pricing need to keep abreast of trends and fads. They also need to know as much as possible about new developments that could affect their clients. New equipment, new standards for food safety, new products all have to be at the tip of the tongue to keep clients. Attending food shows and conventions is one way to keep abreast. Reading industry magazines and newsletters is another. But consultants need to look farther afield, too.

Happenings in the business world, arts and entertainment, and politics all have an impact, too.

Food photographers and stylists should actively seek out not only the most au courant publications. They need additional training in the tricks of the trade, and they may attend special workshops or seminars that focus on special problems or opportunities in their fields. Dining in restaurants, scouring flea markets, and watching food-related television and Web-based programs are part of the equation as well.

Recipe developers and testers, like photographers, stylists, and consultants, have to know what the latest trend is in cooking. They need to develop a network of sources for exotic, unusual, and out-of-season products. Equipment needs may vary from project to project. The ability to operate a new machine is just as important as finding an unusual edible flower to garnish a salad.

All of these factors—planning, perseverance, keeping abreast of new developments—combined with maintaining your love of food and a commitment to quality will help you realize your dream career in the delicious world of food.

Organizations for Food Service Professionals

American Culinary Federation (ACF)
10 San Bartola Drive
St. Augustine, FL 32085
www.acfchefs.org

American Institute of Wine and Food (AIWF)
304 West Liberty Street, Suite 201
Louisville, KY 40202
www.aiwf.org

International Association of Culinary Professionals (IACP)
304 West Liberty Street, Suite 201
Louisville, KY 40202
www.iacp.com

The James Beard Foundation
167 West Twelfth Street
New York, NY 10011
www.jamesbeard.org

National Restaurant Association
1200 Seventeenth Street NW
Washington, DC 20036
www.restaurant.org

Professional Cooking Schools

Academy of Culinary Arts
Atlantic Community College
5100 Black Horse Pike
Mays Landing, NJ 08330
www.atlantic.edu

Boston University Seminars in the Culinary Arts
Metropolitan College
755 Commonwealth Avenue, Suite B-3
Boston, MA 02215
www.bu.edu/met/continuing_ed/lifelong/seminars.html

California Culinary Academy
625 Polk Street
San Francisco, CA 94102
www.baychef.com

Clark College Culinary Arts Department
1800 East McLoughlin Boulevard
Vancouver, WA 98663
www.clark.edu

The Culinary Institute of America
1946 Campus Drive
Hyde Park, NY 12538
www.ciachef.edu

The Culinary School of Kendall College
2408 Orrington Avenue
Evanston, IL 60201
www.kendall.edu

The French Culinary Institute
462 Broadway
New York, NY 10013
www.frenchculinary.com

Johnson and Wales University
Culinary Arts Division
One Washington Avenue
Providence, RI 02905
www.jwu.edu/acad_cul.htm

New England Culinary Institute
250 Main Street
Montpelier, VT 05602
www.neculinary.com

New York Restaurant School
27 West Thirty-fourth Street
New York, NY 10001
www.nyrs.artinstitutes.edu

Scottsdale Culinary Institute
4141 North Scottsdale Road, Suite 110
Scottsdale, AZ 85251
www.scichefs.com/index.php3

Western Culinary Institute
1316 Southwest Thirteenth Avenue
Portland, OR 97201
www.culinaryschools.com/schools/428.htm

Periodicals

Art Culinaire
Culinaire Inc.
40 Mills Street
Morristown, NJ 07960
www.getartc.com

Bon Appétit
5900 Wilshire Boulevard
Los Angeles, CA 90036
www.bonappetit.com

Cooking Light
2100 Lakeshore Drive
Birmingham, AL 35209
www.cookinglight.com

The National Culinary Review
10 Bartola Drive
St. Augustine, FL 32085
www.acfchefs.org

Food Arts
127 East Fifty-Ninth Street
New York, NY 10022

Food & Wine
1120 Avenue of the Americas
New York, NY 10036
www.foodandwine.com

Gourmet
560 Lexington Avenue
New York, NY 10022
www.gourmet.com

Nation's Restaurant News
425 Park Avenue
New York, NY 10022
www.nrn.com

Restaurant Business
770 Broadway
New York, NY 10003
www.foodservicetoday.com

Restaurants & Institutions
1350 East Touhy Avenue
Des Plaines, IL 60017
www.rimag.com

About the Author

Mary Deirdre Donovan has worked in the culinary arts for the past eighteen years. Her first jobs included working at a small country club and, as a student, in a college cafeteria. While earning a bachelor's degree in liberal arts and then pursuing graduate study in philosophy and education, she continued to work for a variety of different restaurants, including a small family-operated delicatessen and a Jack in the Box.

After a year spent teaching grammar to secretarial students in the Philadelphia branch of Katharine Gibbs schools, she found herself ready to make the plunge into the restaurant field. She began as a bartender at a small Pennsylvania inn. When the inn was taken over by a young chef, she was able to assist in all phases of opening up a new business, from preparing foods to planning menus.

From there, she went on to earn an associate's degree in occupational sciences from the Culinary Institute of America in 1983. Since that time, she has worked for the institute as the cookbook editor. Ms. Donovan resides with her family in the Hudson Valley in upstate New York.